FOUL DEEDS & SUSPICIOUS DEATHS IN STRATFORD & SOUTH WARWICKSHIRE

FOUL DEEDS AND SUSPICIOUS DEATHS SERIES

Wharncliffe's *Foul Deeds and Suspicious Deaths* series explores, in detail, crimes of passion, brutal murders and foul misdemeanours from early modern times to the present day. Victorian street crime, mysterious deaths and modern murders tell tales where passion, jealousy and social deprivation brought unexpected violence to those involved. From unexplained death and suicide to murder and manslaughter, the books provide a fascinating insight into the lives of both victims and perpetrators as well as society as a whole.

Other titles in the series include:

Foul Deeds and Suspicious Deaths around Birmingham, Nick Billingham
ISBN: 1-903425-96-4. £10.99

Foul Deeds and Suspicious Deaths in and around Chesterfield, Geoffrey Sadler
ISBN: 1-903425-30-1. £9.99

Foul Deeds and Suspicious Deaths in and around Colchester, Patrick Denny
ISBN: 1-903425-54-9. £10.99

More Foul Deeds and Suspicious Deaths in and around Chesterfield, Geoffrey Sadler
ISBN: 1-903425-68-9. £9.99

Foul Deeds and Suspicious Deaths around Derby, Kevin Turton
ISBN: 1-903425-76-X. £9.99

Foul Deeds and Suspicious Deaths in and around Durham, Maureen Anderson
ISBN: 1-903425-46-8. £9.99

Foul Deeds and Suspicious Deaths in and around Halifax, Stephen Wade
ISBN: 1-903425-45-X. £9.99

Foul Deeds and Suspicious Deaths in Hampstead, Holborn and St Pancras, Mark Aston
ISBN: 1-903425-94-8. £10.99

Foul Deeds and Suspicious Deaths in Leeds, David Goodman
ISBN: 1-903425-08-5. £9.99

Foul Deeds and Suspicious Deaths in London's East End, Geoffrey Howse
ISBN: 1-903425-71-9. £10.99

Foul Deeds and Suspicious Deaths in Manchester, Martin Baggoley
ISBN: 1-903425-65-4. £9.99

Foul Deeds and Suspicious Deaths in and around Mansfield, Geoffrey Sadler
ISBN: 1-903425-67-0. £10.99

Foul Deeds and Suspicious Deaths in Newcastle, Maureen Anderson
ISBN: 1-903425-34-4. £9.99

Foul Deeds and Suspicious Deaths in Nottingham, Kevin Turton
ISBN: 1-903425-35-2. £9.99

Foul Deeds and Suspicious Deaths around Pontefract and Castleford, Keith Henson
ISBN: 1-903425-54-9. £9.99

More Foul Deeds and Suspicious Deaths in Wakefield, Kate Taylor
ISBN: 1-903425-48-4. £9.99

Foul Deeds and Suspicious Deaths in York, Keith Henson
ISBN: 1-903425-33-6. £9.99

Please contact us via any of the methods below for more information or a catalogue.
WHARNCLIFFE BOOKS
47 Church Street – Barnsley – South Yorkshire – S70 2AS
Tel: 01226 734555 – 734222 Fax: 01226 734438
E-mail: enquiries@pen-and-sword.co.uk – Website: www.wharncliffebooks.co.uk

Foul Deeds & Suspicious Deaths in

STRATFORD & SOUTH WARWICKSHIRE

NICK BILLINGHAM

Series Editor
Brian Elliott

Wharncliffe Books

This book is dedicated
to John Corvin

First Published in Great Britain in 2006 by
Wharncliffe Books
an imprint of
Pen and Sword Books Ltd
47 Church Street
Barnsley
South Yorkshire
S70 2AS

Copyright © Nick Billingham, 2006

ISBN: 1-903425-99-9

Typeset in 11/13pt Plantin by Mac Style, Nafferton, E. Yorkshire.

Printed and bound in England by CPI UK.

Pen and Sword Books Ltd incorporates the Imprints of
Pen & Sword Aviation, Pen & Sword Maritime,
Pen & Sword Military, Wharncliffe Books,
Pen & Sword Select, Pen and Sword Military Classics
and Leo Cooper.

For a complete list of Pen & Sword titles please contact
PEN & SWORD BOOKS LIMITED
47 Church Street
Barnsley
South Yorkshire
S70 2BR
England
E-mail: enquiries@pen-and-sword.co.uk
Website: www.pen-and-sword.co.uk

Contents

Charlotte Clopton, entombed in the crypt. Strand Magazine

Acknowledgements

I would like to extend my heartfelt thanks to Dr Bearman and all the staff at the Shakespeare Birthplace Trust Records Office for their invaluable help. Warwickshire County Records Office also deserve my thanks for the splendid service they provide. Thanks to my family for putting up with the mountains of paperwork across the dining room table and my friends for listening to endless tales of local horrors.

Introduction

Stratford-upon-Avon basks in the limelight of international fame these days. It projects an image of culture and industry and is a pretty civilised place to live. The town seems to be a peaceful and wealthy market with an additional cosmopolitan atmosphere that all our overseas visitors bring with them. Life is not all roses though. Even in Stratford there have been jealousies, feuds and sheer stupidity. The resulting mayhem is documented in this collection of the less savoury incidents of the town's history. These are the tales that didn't make it into the tourist brochures, or the estate agents' blurbs.

The stories start back in the mists of time and end fifty years ago. This isn't because the locals have suddenly become good

These days Henley Street is the centre of an international tourist trade. Christmas 1795 saw a running battle between the townsfolk and a platoon of Dragoons in the White Lion. The author

citizens; we've had plenty of murders in the last half-century. However, I do not intend to re-open wounds that have barely healed; fifty years is about right to find a sense of perspective and allows both victims and murderers to find their place in the unfolding tapestry of history. As I have been acquainted with a couple of our more recent cases, I would have to admit a personal bias, which wouldn't do at all.

Murders are all unique, a particular set of unfortunate circumstances that result in the usually unexpected death of someone or other. Stratford seems to have more than its fair share of unsolved ones. The Meon Hill murder remains a complete mystery. The complete failure of the police to find the culprit has led to a whole host of strange stories; allegations of witchcraft and black magic are rife and so much more interesting than a simple grudge killing. The case has entered occult folklore and if you try researching the matter you have to overcome a mountain of superstitious twaddle before you get to the facts. However, Meon Hill is a very special place, so the mystery has a momentum all of its own.

The murder of Olive Bennet is also unsolved. As with the Meon Hill case, there are plenty of people who feel they know

From the middle of the seventeenth century Stratford was a busy market town that used river transport and the network of roads built by the Romans. The workers on the river led a secret and often criminal life. Shakespeare Birthplace Trust Records Office

Samuel Ireland drew this view of the town during his travels along the Avon in 1795. The town became famous for its Shakespeare connections after the Grand Jubilee of 1769. Life for the ordinary citizen remained just as difficult despite the new tourist trade. Shakespeare Birthplace Trust Records Office

the identity of the culprit. Some of them may even be right, but without hard and fast evidence the legal case cannot be proven. If we started arresting people on the evidence of the local grapevine – Stratford would probably be deserted!

Murder can take many forms; letting rip with a hatchet is straightforward enough but what about the sad cases where vulnerable people have died because those who were entrusted with their care neglected their duty? Stratford has a simply appalling record in this respect. Sad little bodies have been dragged from the river, murdered before they were even named. Starving mothers left to die alone in a dank workhouse cell. Our civic history is not entirely without blemish.

As we peer further back into our history there are subtle changes. Wherever possible I quote people's speech exactly as it was recorded. It looks a little odd on the page, but if you read the words aloud, you will gain an insight into the accent and speech patterns of our ancestors. Even the spelling mistakes (theirs not mine) give you a clue as to the way people spoke the language. Unfortunately we can only do this for a few centuries; further back the evidence becomes hazy and indistinct. Some of the town's most grisly tales come from so far back that they can only really be considered legends. There simply isn't the evidence to prove that they really happened, but what writer could possibly ignore the curse of the Cloptons just because of a little detail like that?

Even further back there is nothing but archaeological evidence and such murders can only point out a dim and misty picture of a world utterly different to our own, apart, of course, from a common tendency to let rip with a hatchet.

It isn't easy working out which is the first murder for Stratford. Back in the 1790s some workmen unearthed a

skeleton whose skull had an arrow head embedded in it. The skeleton seems to be from the Iron Age, long before the Romans arrived, but was it a murder? An arrow in the head seems to be part of an act of warfare rather than a typical domestic dispute. The skeleton was unearthed near 'Castle Hill' on the Welcombe estate, a very ancient site. The trouble is that the archaeology of the eighteenth century was a bit primitive and we know very little

The citizens of Stratford have often resorted to violence in difficult times. The mills on the river were broken open by the starving poor on several occasions. Strand Magazine

surrounding the fact of a skull with an arrow in it. It is debatable whether there was even a Stratford at the time.

Stratford's first murder seems to have been at Tiddington in about AD 480. A body was carelessly thrown into a ditch. The decapitated corpse was just left to rot in the open. Such a callous end to someone's life cannot be explained in personal detail, but perhaps the circumstances around the event can shed a little light on this first dark deed.

The Saxon invasion got into top gear with the disappearance of the Roman Legions. Sporadic resistance took place and legend tells of a vast battle between the Britons and West Saxons in AD 584. The exact location of the battle is unknown, but one possible place is at Milcote, just south of Stratford. In this battle the West Saxons, led by Caelwin and Cutha, defeated the British to extend their lands northwards from Gloucestershire. The clues are few, a Saxon charter mentions a place called 'Fachanleah', meaning battlefield, another and more significant clue to the battle appeared when in 1866 an excavation beside the River Stour just beside the site of Milcote Manor revealed over 400 skeletons crammed into an area of only 100 square feet. They were all adults and all buried without the usual grave goods or weapons. It seems that further excavations will reveal even more skeletons. Is this mass grave on the site of the penultimate battle between the British and the Saxons? The vanquished warriors stripped and thrown into a shallow grave beside the river.

The little British village, surrounded by its defensive ditch was under constant threat. Saxon invaders were working their way across the Midland plain and our British ancestors seem to have hired German mercenaries for extra protection. It was to be to no avail, the Germans settled close to the Roman ford, and the village at Tiddington gradually became a deserted ruin. The two communities shared a cemetery for a while, but in the end the German mercenaries probably had a lot more in common with the Saxon invaders. In an era of raids and pillage, a nameless corpse thrown into the ditch of an abandoned village was quite unremarkable. The nettles and willowherb grew wild across the site until there was nothing left to ever show that this was the birthplace of our town.

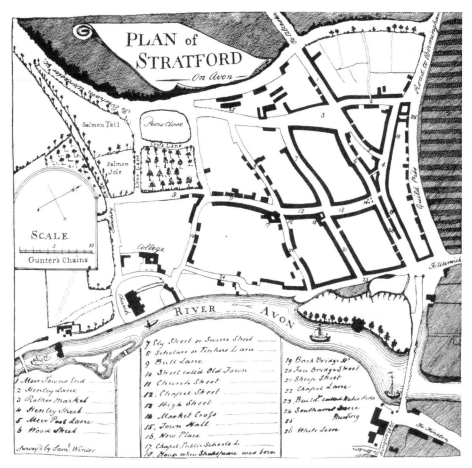

Samuel Winter drew the first map of the town centre in 1765. Research has shown that the town shrank by a third after the Black Death and did not recover for five centuries. Shakespeare Birthplace Trust Records Office

Without documentary evidence these very early murders can only be pure speculation; after the Middle Ages there are detailed records of virtually every crime and it is from these records that this book is drawn. Court cases, coroners' inquests and contemporary newspapers all open up a unique insight into the real world of history. It is a place full of ordinary people and, just like today, extraordinary events.

People ask me if I know how to commit the perfect murder after all this research. Well, no, most of these stories are the direct result of someone getting caught. What I have learnt is that the most likely person to kill you is your spouse or lover. Be nice to your better half, check that they haven't taken out extra life insurance on you and don't forget to hide the hatchet; preferably somewhere where you can get to it in a hurry.

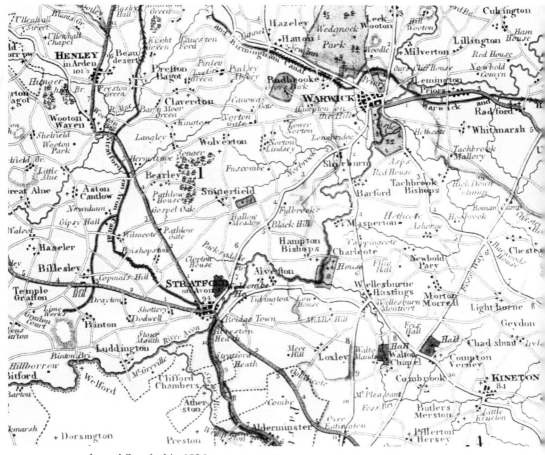

Around Stratford in 1826. Author's collection

CHAPTER 1

The Clopton Horror
1564

An absolute horror was revealed in the flickering lamplight.

The further back in time one looks, the more vague and indistinct the events become. A few centuries back and there are no newspaper accounts, further back still, there are no prosecution papers and even the records of births, marriages and deaths become unreliable. Accurate history becomes folklore and hearsay and you really can't be too sure what actually happened, or even if it happened at all. There simply isn't enough evidence to make a firm opinion. Nevertheless some events were so dramatic that they carved a permanent place into the memories of Stratfordians. Nowhere is more embedded in the local folklore than Clopton House. Psychics and sensationalist television programmes not withstanding, it is a very odd place that seems to have laboured under a curse for many generations. There has been a farm or house there since Saxon times and who knows what dark deeds took place before recorded history.

In 1564 Stratford was not the place to be. An epidemic of plague was sweeping through the population. In the days before modern medicine all sorts of infectious diseases were called plague, and Stratford seems to have been infected with 'English Sweating Sickness' rather than the more usual Bubonic variety:

A newe Kynde of sickness came through the whole region, which was so sore, so peynfull, and sharp, that the lyke was never harde of to any mannes rememberance before that tyme.

The Clopton family at Clopton House may have hoped that their wealthy seclusion would keep them safe, but just like the

Edgar Allen Poe story, *The Masque of the Red Death*, the disease found a way in. The young Charlotte Clopton,

> *a sweet-looking girl, with paly gold hair combed back from her forehead and falling in wavy ringlets on her neck, and with eyes that 'looked like violets filled with dew,' for there was the glittering of unshed tears before their deep dark blue,*

contracted the awful sickness. She gradually weakened and slipped into a deep death-like coma. Unfortunately for Charlotte it was a little too like death, and given the dire emergency of the plague, the family whipped her into a coffin and hastily removed the body to the family crypt at Holy Trinity Church. That should have been that, but the plague continued to devastate the townspeople and a week or so later another member of the Clopton family died of the disease. They were duly placed in a coffin and the sorry funeral party once again heaved open the doors to the crypt and descended the cold stone stairs into the darkness.

An absolute horror was revealed in the flickering lamplight. Charlotte had woken inside her coffin, struggled out in the pitch-blackness and tried to escape. Her thirst was growing with every passing hour. She bit into her shoulder to try to drink her own blood. Still attempting to escape, her bleeding fingers dug into the ancient stonework, scrabbling frantically for air and light. The days passed in the silent darkness as her strength ebbed away. Finally, standing with her fingers clawing at a promising crevice between the stones, she died.

The mourners found her still standing there. The news spread quickly through the town and people were still talking about it years later. During those years a local lad with a penchant for writing heard the story and used the idea in his play Romeo and Juliet. Edgar Allen Poe based The Fall of the House of Usher story on the tale too. The Clopton family had not finished providing literary inspiration yet though.

Margaret Clopton was born in 1563, luckily surviving the plague that killed twenty per cent of Stratfordians. By the 1590s she was a grown woman and had fallen passionately in love. The lad however doesn't seem to have been quite so fond of her and jilted her. Margaret wandered around Clopton House bewailing her fate, and generally losing the plot. Eventually, so legend has it, she jumped in the well and drowned herself. This was seriously inconvenient as no one wanted to drink the water any more, and they had to dig another well. Margaret's Well went out of use and became overgrown. It was considered to be part fable until a couple of years ago when the well was rediscovered during some drainage work. Margaret is reputed to be the inspiration for Ophelia in Shakespeare's *Hamlet*.

I need hardly add that both Charlotte and Margaret's unquiet spirits roam the ancient corridors and rooms of Clopton House, along with a spectral murderer and quite possibly a black dog or two. The house itself has yet more dark connotations though.

The Gunpowder Plot of 1605, when a group of Catholics tried to blow up the House of Commons and the King, had very strong local connections. The rural Warwickshire gentry maintained their old faith and Catholic customs long after the town had become Protestant. By now the Clopton family had shrunk and been forced to rent out the house. Hardly surprising considering the sticky ends they all seemed to be meeting. A wealthy young man by the name of Ambrose Rockwood rented the somewhat dilapidated pile. Depending on your point of view he was either a member of a group of dedicated religious idealists fighting for their right to practice their faith in peace, or one of a bunch of vicious terrorists who planned to overthrow English society by killing as many innocent people as they could and force an alien religion upon them.

Ambrose had two passions in life, the Catholic faith and racing horses. In 1604, when in his early twenties, he had obtained a large quantity of gunpowder for an acquaintance of his, Catesby. Catesby lived in Lapworth, then a part of Stratford. It seems he was unaware that Catesby was part of a small cabal plotting something spectacular. In the early autumn of 1605 Ambrose was told of the plot and became an enthusiastic supporter. Catesby told him to rent somewhere safe, and he chose Clopton House. He excavated a secret underground chamber, complete with escape tunnel, to house a small altar and chalices. Clopton House became one of a series of 'safe houses' that the conspirators intended to use as centres of a general insurrection.

On 31 October, Ambrose rode down to London to see how the plot was advancing. He might have thought that they were on the verge of a great rebellion with Catholics emerging to join the armed struggle once the explosion took place, but even as he was being given a grand sword with 'Passion of Christ' engraved on it, the plot was compromised and he was a doomed man. He was one of the last conspirators to be tipped off that the game was up. He leapt on a horse and galloped hell for leather towards the Midlands. His prowess as one of the country's fastest horsemen was well founded and he soon caught up with Catesby and the others who had fled earlier.

In London Guy Fawkes was being tortured to reveal the names of the plotters. Rockwood's name came out and instructions were sent post-haste to Stratford to seize and search Clopton House. An armed group of citizens piled out of the pub and stormed the house. There were no conspirators there so they ransacked it. They found the secret chambers and religious paraphernalia, but of Rockwood there was no sign.

Rockwood was on the run with the others. They were sheltered at Hewell Grange where they obtained some money and a barrel of gunpowder. From there they rode through the rain to Holbeach House near Kingswinford. There they tried to dry themselves out, and in an act of sheer breathtaking stupidity, decided to dry the gunpowder out by spreading it on the floor in front of the fire. The inevitable explosion blinded one of them and badly burnt the rest. It alerted the local militia and in the resulting gunfight a musket ball hit Ambrose. Burnt and wounded he was captured and transferred to London. He was stuck in the Tower of London long enough to engrave his name into the wall of Martin Tower, and interrogated at length. On 27 January 1606 he was put on trial for high treason, and sentenced to death. He pleaded for clemency in a moving speech, but it did him no good. On the 31st he was tied to a

Clopton House. Shakespeare Birthplace Trust Records Office

hurdle and dragged through the streets of London to Westminster. He managed to call out 'Pray for me' to his wife Elizabeth and then he was hung, drawn and quartered. It was a particularly ghastly way to die.

Clopton House was once again vacant. The plot gave Shakespeare more inspiration and ideas about politics. Strangely enough the house's contribution to English literature was still not complete. The gruesome tales inspired John Jordan to write them down in the 1790s and in the 1820s the budding novelist Elizabeth Gaskell visited the place. Her account of the place and the description of the portrait of Charlotte quoted above helped put her in the top league of English writers of the day.

CHAPTER 2

The Killing of Joseph Pinfield
1795
... he sank to his knees crying 'Oh Lord' over and over again.

S tratford in the 1790s was gradually growing into the town that we know today. The town had lain stagnant for centuries after the devastation of the Black Death in 1349 but from about 1750 things really started to pick up. There was a new spirit abroad and the ordinary citizens started to take charge of their own destiny. The people rather than the patriarchal government drove ambitious projects like the improvements to the roads or the creation of the canal system. In England this mood led to the Industrial Revolution. In France it led to an altogether different sort of revolution.

These days Hell Lane is called Windsor Street. It was at the corner with Rother Street that some townsfolk attacked the soldiers, triggering a night of violence. The author

The town had often been forced to billet platoons of soldiers. It was never an easy process. The people of the town resented this intrusion intensely. In 1765 the squad billeted on the town were blamed for an outbreak of smallpox that killed dozens of people. The outbreak of war with France meant that more soldiers were sent to the town. Nominally for our protection, but in reality the government of the day was quietly terrified that the English would follow the French and overthrow the monarchy and all the institutions that depended on it. It seemed touch and go for a while; but when the French killed their king, the English rallied behind George III. Oddly enough, he was a surprisingly popular monarch. The troops remained in the town though; a constant drain on the borough.

The county raised its own Yeomanry Regiment in 1794, comprised of local respectable men. It was commanded by Captain James Shirley and was also a direct result of the fears of civil unrest. These men were living in their own homes and called to arms as required. Captain Shirley lived at Ettington Park, so the regiment was not capable of the fastest response. In the town itself The Fifth Regiment of Dragoons had been billeted in the pubs, with a guardroom and headquarters at the *White Lion* in Henley Street. They were anything but welcome.

The owner of the *White Lion* was John Payton. He was one of a group of dynamic men who were exerting all their energies into making Stratford a wealthy town. They were starting to exploit the Shakespeare connection, and John Payton was offering the first Shakespeare tours. The very last thing he needed was for his pub to be crowded with a bunch of loud-mouthed Irish Troopers for months on end. Throughout the autumn of 1795 tensions mounted between the townsfolk and the soldiers.

By Christmas Day 1795 tempers were getting more than a little frayed. The soldiers were probably feeling homesick and consoled themselves with plenty of beer. The simplest way to achieve this was to go on 'patrol' around the town, taking a particular interest in the pubs. The landlords were used to this unofficial taxation and were heartily sick of it. As it was

The pub is called the Old Thatch Tavern *today, since it is the last thatched building in the town. All the houses used to be thatched, but most of them burnt down in a series of catastrophic fires during the seventeenth century. The* Old Thatch Tavern *is a lucky survivor.* The author

Christmas, most of the townspeople had been celebrating too. The last thing they wanted was their Christmas get-togethers interrupted by a bunch of Dragoons bullying their way to the bar to harass a free beer out of the landlord. By early evening the town was just about ready to explode.

The first signs of trouble happened around teatime; Thomas Carnall was walking along the street past a group of soldiers when he was knocked to the ground by one of them. They growled at him that they would serve all the men in the town the same way. They struck out at another man, James

Warrilow, as well. Strutting around the town in their red regimental uniforms, they may have felt themselves invincible. George Ward and a friend certainly thought so as they were chased around the town by half a dozen of them. George eventually managed to hide himself in the hayloft above the stables of the *White Lion*.

Mr Bolton was just one of the landlords of the town pubs who was thoroughly fed up of them; as Christmas evening wore on he had Troopers Cain, Quin, and Fitzgerald arguing with each other and going into his kitchen to help themselves to his beer. Needless to say they weren't offering to pay for it.

Captain Sherlock sent out a patrol at 9 o'clock. It was Patrick Welch's duty to see that all the troopers were in their quarters. It can't have been too onerous a task, checking every single pub in the town! He managed to get back to the guardhouse to make his report at half nine, and presumably staggered back to his quarters at the *Malt Shovel*.

Meer Street was lined with small houses and gardens in 1795. Very few of these buildings still survive. The author

Elizabeth Baker, the landlady of the *Malt Shovel*, (today called the *Old Thatch Tavern*) refused to serve Welch any more beer, saying it was too late. Welch decided that despite orders for all the soldiers to be in their quarters, he was going for a drink elsewhere, and made his way to the *Shakespeare* to join Cain, Fitzgerald and Quin. There Quin tried to persuade him not to drink any more, but he flew in a rage and went into the kitchen to help himself to a pot, James Fitzgerald and Hugh Kelly joined him, leaving Quin alone.

Out in the streets the Christmas revelries were winding down and a tense peace settling in. Gradually the various townspeople were going to bed or gathering in their houses over a late supper. There were still people drinking in the pubs, particularly the *Malt Shovel*.

At midnight Corporal Ridley led the next patrol; he had James Anderson and Patrick Welch with him. They left the guardhouse and walked down Hell Lane (today called Windsor Street). As they reached the market place they walked into a small group of locals coming out of the *Malt Shovel*. A fight broke out and the trooper James Anderson got thoroughly beaten up. Ridley himself had received a hefty blow. John Broom, one of the locals was also hurt but managed to escape with the help of Matthew Hiron. It was a brief skirmish and John and Matthew seem to have run back into the *Malt Shovel* through the back door when they realised fists were no match against the swords and nightsticks of an army patrol. Corporal Ridley and Patrick Welch weren't going to let the matter rest there though. Ridley may well have been sober, but it seems that Welch was fighting drunk.

Ridley told Welch and Anderson to go in through the back door whilst he took the front. Welch kicked in the back door and proceeded to smash up the kitchen, knocking plates and dishes off the shelves to smash on the floor. No doubt he wanted a bit of revenge for having been refused a beer earlier. Anderson wasn't much help here, it seems he sat by the back door bruised and battered from his first encounter.

Corporal Ridley battered open the front door hoping to find his assailants, but only met Thomas Baker, the landlord, and his wife. He seized Baker and called for Anderson and Welch to come and hold him. Elizabeth Baker was screaming 'Murder' at the top of her voice. Corporal Ridley found things getting out of hand and ran back to the guardhouse to get trooper Howard and a few others. They ran back to the *Malt Shovel* and decided to take their prisoner into custody. Anderson and Welch were ordered to take Baker to the upstairs room at the headquarters. The rest of the soldiers remained in the market place.

Elizabeth Baker stopped screaming murder and went to fetch Constable Buller, telling him how the soldiers had broken open their house and taken her husband away. He understood the gravity of the situation and called at several people's houses to make up a reasonable force. William Fletcher, another of the town's constables, refused to get out of bed, saying he was ill. Abraham West also refused to get out of bed. Constable John Hitchman joined Buller as did several ordinary citizens, Joseph Pinfield, Matthew Hiron, John Broom and William Buck.

The soldiers in the market place were now out of control. James Cheshire was in his house with his neighbours, William Smith, Thomas Carnall and his wife. No doubt they had discussed the atrocious behaviour of the troopers as they sat down to dinner, but they really didn't expect what happened next. James heard Elizabeth's cries of murder and looked out of his window to see four or five soldiers in the yard brandishing drawn swords. Very quietly he fastened his door, hoping that they would go on past. They didn't. The door was smashed open and they rushed into the house and started attacking every one in it. James received several cuts to the head, as did Thomas. Two of the soldiers grabbed a pair of mattock staves as weapons and chased the terrified Thomas Carnall out of the house and down the street. Thomas didn't stop running until he reached the fields outside the town where he cowered in terror for the rest of the night.

The soldiers ransacked James Cheshire's house. They then smashed all the windows in Thomas Bolt's house nearby. Rother Street was starting to look like a war zone as the two soldiers who chased Thomas Carnall returned and searched for any more money in James's house.

The scene of the murder of Joseph Pinfield. In 1795 Meer Street was known as Mere Pool Lane since it contained a pond that allowed the cattle in the market to get a drink. The author

At the guardhouse Captain Sherlock was getting out of his depth. The midnight patrol had returned battered and bloody, called for help and most of the off duty soldiers had then grabbed their swords and run out. They left Henry Bryan, who had been drinking with them, wondering what on earth was happening. He decided it would be wise to drink up and clear off home. Upstairs, Mary Field, one of the servants, was alarmed at the sudden exodus. Out in the yard George Ward was still hiding in the hayloft. He saw the soldiers rush out and ducked down behind the trapdoor. Minutes later the patrol returned with a bruised prisoner. Ridley dragged Baker into the soldier's room and smashed him across the face with the flat of his sword. Anderson slumped down onto his bed, particularly bruised. John Davis, who was another servant at the *White Lion*, went outside to see what the commotion was about. There he met a man, woman and child. The man had been cut about the face and was bleeding badly. As the sorry little family passed on into the night John decided it would be best to lock up the *Lion*. He dragged the heavy gates closed and locked them.

Constable Buller had managed to raise a small force of townspeople to try and find Thomas Baker. They went into one of the town gardens and armed themselves with sticks from the woodpile and fence stakes. As they came into the market place they met the soldiers at the corner of Hell Lane. On both sides the simmering hostility of the last few months was all set to boil over.

Trooper James Kelly had been interrupted from his dalliance with the 'common girl' Miss Kitty in a hovel at the back of the *Malt Shovel*, so no doubt he was in a filthy temper. Patrick Welch seems to have returned to the *Malt Shovel* to scrounge another pot of beer by assuring Elizabeth Baker that Thomas would be alright. He wasn't that sober to start with. Corporal Ridley had been humiliated by a bunch of ordinary citizens, Trooper Howard had got a bleeding nose and another trooper, Samuel Irwin, seems to have tagged along for the fight. The troopers took one look at Constable Buller's little army and pounced on them with drawn swords.

It was anything but an even fight. The troopers were in their regimental red dress, armed with standard issue broadswords; and they knew exactly how to use them. The townsfolk had sticks, still with the bark on them. Constable Buller called out 'Peace' at the top of his voice, but the soldiers' blood was up and they paid no heed.

They shouted back, 'By their Dear Jesus and the Holy Ghost they would massacre the first man they laid hold of'. Even before the two sides clashed, John Hitchman took one look at the armed soldiers and bolted for home. Matthew Hiron found himself facing a naked sword held by a soldier threatening to cut his entrails out if he came near. James Warrilow had got up to join them but his wife dragged him back to his home in Mere Pool Lane (now Meer Street). Buller, Willam Buck, John Broom and Joseph Pinfield charged into the fray. It was madness really, within seconds William Buck was battered and bruised, a sudden swipe of a broadsword had nearly killed him and cut right through his hat; he turned and ran to a safer distance. John Broom struggled in the melee until he was caught by one of the dragoons. As he squirmed to escape, the dragoon called to his friend, Paddy, for help. John managed to wriggle free and bolted for cover.

Constable Buller and Joseph Pinfield fought on. Buller was taking more and more cuts from the swords until he could bear no more and ran. Pinfield was now alone amid the five furious soldiers. They slashed at him repeatedly with their swords as he sank to his knees crying 'Oh Lord' over and over again. Rebecca, his wife, now charged into the fray and pulled him up. Astonished, the soldiers seem to have held back as she dragged him along in front of the *Kings Head* and into their house in Mere Pool Lane.

Kelly started to chase them, with Welch and Irwin close behind. Rebecca slammed and bolted the door while Joseph staggered out into the back garden to attempt to hide. Kelly, Welch and Irwin shouted 'By their Dear Jesus and Holy Ghost they would massacre him'; then they smashed open the door and charged through the house. They found Joseph lying on the ground and attacked him again.

Rebecca screamed and pleaded for mercy, but they slashed and stabbed at Joseph with their swords. Welch and Irwin tired, and pulled Kelly off saying 'Damn your soul, do you mean to kill the man?'

Kelly wrenched himself free and shouted 'He'll do better for another blow' and made one last furious assault on Joseph, striking his head so hard that he bent his sword. It was more than enough to kill Joseph.

James Warrilow looked out of his window in horror at the attack. The soldiers came out of the garden, Kelly brandishing his sword over his head calling to the others, asking, 'Did you ever see it work so well before?' They said they had not and proceeded to kick in the door of the house next to him. James cowered in utter fear as they ransacked the widow's house and then tried his own door. As they rattled the handle they called out that they would murder everyone inside. Fortunately for the Warrilow family, the door held fast and they wandered off towards the guardhouse.

Abraham West had also watched the attack from his house. He had managed to sleep through most of the debacle, but Rebecca's shrieks of Murder had woken him. He watched from his window as she pleaded for her husband's life, to no avail.

As the soldiers left Sarah Buck crept out of her house and went across the road to see what had happened to Rebecca and Joseph Pinfield.

In less than an hour the town had been changed from a peaceful market town enjoying a tranquil Christmas to a scene of major civil unrest. A rider was despatched to call up the local militia of Captain James Shirley but it would be hours before they could arrive. Most of the town's constables were battered and cut about in the fighting and the Dragoons officers seem to have been clueless as to the events unfolding around them. Captain Redwood seems to have been unaware that Corporal Ridley had taken a prisoner since Ridley had reported to Captain Sherlock. Both of them seem to have been in the *White Lion* when Baker was brought in, but Redwood appears to have missed the action and wandered off to his lodgings with the Fletchers at about the time Rebecca was screaming for her husband's life.

When he got back Mrs Fletcher soon told him what was going on, and had got her husband out of bed too. Redwood was very agitated and admitted he had heard the cry of Murder. They decided they had to go out and attempt to restore order, Redwood had left his sword at the guardhouse, and so he armed himself with a poker. As they stepped out into the night they bumped into Mrs Smith. Asking her if she had seen any soldiers she told them there were none in her yard and they carried on towards the guardhouse. Mary Field in the *White Lion* watched as Captain Redwood walked down the street. He kept to the shadows, walking very gently as though frightened to meet his own anarchic soldiers. She called down to John Davis to open the door for him as he crossed the road in front of her. Davis opened up, but Redwood had slunk off further along the street towards the Post Office.

Redwood and Constable Fletcher met up with Ridley, Howard, Irwin and two privates, possibly Kelly and Welch. Ridley told him the gist of what had happened at the *Malt Shovel* and they all went to the guardhouse. Captain Redwood then took Howard, Welch and Irwin with him to the *Malt*

Shovel to survey the wreckage. By now news of the murder was out and they went to the Pinfields' house where he found a distraught Rebecca being comforted by Sarah Buck and Joseph lying dead in the garden. With an almost supreme indifference, he then told the soldiers to go back to their quarters and he himself went back to his lodgings to go to bed.

Sarah Buck decided to get a pot of beer for Rebecca. The *Malt Shovel* was ablaze with lights as Elizabeth paced about fretting over her imprisoned husband. The house was in a dreadful state with shattered windows and the shards of plates all over the floor. Sarah asked Elizabeth for a jug of beer and waited. She noticed one soldier sitting there quietly and soon another four came in. Three of them were carrying swords and the other a large stick. To her horror and disgust she saw that their swords and trousers were all covered in blood. Fitzgerald told them to sit down and be quiet. They drank quietly; their killing rage had now worn off.

It was now about two in the morning. George Ward had been so thoroughly terrified that he was still in the hayloft above the *Lion* yard. Corporal Ridley climbed over the back gate, clutching two bludgeons and disappeared off in the direction of Captain Sherlock's room. A little while later George saw two soldiers come out to the pump in the yard. One of them, he thought it was Welch, was having plenty of water pumped over him by the other. George clearly heard him say 'Did you see what a bloody thump I gave the rogue?' Henry Bryan was still about the town, he had cleared out of the *White Lion* when the soldiers had poured out, then bumped into the patrol returning with Baker and now he was just outside the *Lion* when he walked into Kelly. Kelly was a right mess, his clothes filthy and he was clutching his sword; it was very bent. Bryan must have looked startled, but Kelly shook him by the hand and promised not to hurt him. Bryan watched him go into the yard and wash himself at the pump. It had been a long day.

Boxing Day dawned to a town shattered by the tragedy. The local militia arrived and soon the dragoons were rounded up and held in their quarters. Thirty local men were appointed special constables and armed properly. The local surgeon,

Thomas Nott, had his work cut out for him over the following few days, stitching up the numerous wounded people. The Overseers of the Poor decided that they would pay for the medical expenses of those injured in the fighting. The bill came to £6 13s 6d, a huge sum for the time.

The coroner's inquest into the night took place in the town hall on 28 December. The body of Joseph Pinfield was lying on the table in front of the accused. Ridley, Welch, Anderson, Irwin, Kelly and Howard were arrested and committed for trial at Warwick Assizes. Ridley's evidence was particularly confused and contradictory and it wasn't until March, when Welch and Irwin decided to make confessions that any real clues to the events became clear.[1] Their confessions do seem slightly forced and they clearly discussed their stories together before committing themselves. Unfortunately the records of their subsequent fates have been lost.

Note
1. See Appendix for full transcription of the two confessions.

CHAPTER 3

The Poor Law Tragedies
1801 onwards
She was now a half-starved wreck ...

At the end of the eighteenth century the Borough of Stratford continued to care for the poor and needy of the town by using money from the Poor Rates. It was a basic tenet of English Society that no one should starve and Parish Relief was designed to prevent absolute poverty by providing almshouses and financial assistance. In some cases money was used to provide apprenticeships for the children of the very poor families.

An apprenticeship allowed a child to learn a trade and, after many years, join the trade guild and earn a good wage. The practice of swapping children between families of craftsmen had been established since the Middle Ages and on the whole it worked well. It has often been remarked by foreigners that the English tend to treat their animals better than their children and, without adequate supervision, this farming out of children had its drawbacks.

The Trustees of Stratford's Poor Law had a rather chequered record when it came to placing poor children into apprenticeships. Most of them returned to their home long before the seven years training was over. In the case of Mary Orton things went dreadfully wrong.

Mary was placed in the care of Thomas and Elizabeth Clark. Thomas was a ribbon-weaver who lived at Ansley near Coventry. When Mary was about twelve the trustees paid him a substantial sum of money to train and care for her. The money was supposed to pay for all her food and board as well as the various costs involved in training and entering her into the local weavers' guild. They didn't check whether this couple were really appropriate; it was an expedient way of getting rid of one of the poor children of the town, apparently a noble deed.

Two years later Thomas and Elizabeth were charged with the attempted murder of Mary Orton. She was now a half-starved wreck with broken bones and hovering on the edge of death. The charge sheet read out in court started thus:

Thos Clark, ribbon weaver and Elizabeth, his wife, persons of wicked, barbarous inhuman, diabolical disposition, on the 1st September 1801 did with force and arms in open, Mary Orton, an infant of about 14 years, Parish Apprentice, assault with whips and sticks, violently scourge and strike Mary. Feloniously, wilfully and of malice aforethought to kill and murder, to the extreme pain, torture and anguish of Mary Orton.

If the couple thought that they could wriggle out of this by appealing to the jury, they had a shock:

One of the jurors do further present that on 21 October and divers other days Thos Clark did barbarously, cruelly and inhumanly neglect and refuse to administer, or permit to be administered, sufficient meat, drink, victuals and other necessities proper and requisite for the sustenance, support and maintenance of the body of her.

It wasn't simply a matter of neglect either, the juror continued:

Then and there force and compel Mary Orton to eat noxious unwholesome foul mixture composed of water and grudgeon [a fresh water fish] whereby Mary became sick and greatly distempered in her body so great that the excrement of the body came involuntarily from her. Thos Clark, with force and arms, with dire threats and menaces wickedly, inhumanly and barbarously did compel and oblige Mary Orton to eat and swallow the same.

Mary survived this ghastly ordeal only to be attacked again:

Thos Clark and Elizabeth his wife did on the 21st December make assault on Mary. Then and there they did beat bruise wound and ill treat her so that her life was greatly despaired of.

Mary was finally brought home and the Clarks sent to prison. The system of Parish Apprenticeships started to decline as a result of incidents like this.

A century passed and the system of Parish apprenticeships and relief to the poor in their own homes was abolished. In a radical reorganisation during the 1830s all parish relief was to be administered within a local workhouse. The old, weak and infirm were incarcerated within the dark utilitarian walls of these places to perform menial tasks in return for a meagre diet and shelter. Homeless families were split up with the women and children going to one ward, the men to another. The workhouses contained nurses and superintendents to ensure a minimum of medical care. Small villages that could not afford to build their own workhouse were permitted to join a Union of other villages and towns to create large institutions. The quality of care varied from town to town. Stratford was a long way from the top of the list when it came to looking after the poor of the district. In several instances their care amounted to nothing less than institutional manslaughter.

The workhouse in Arden Street had the knowledge and resources to be able to cater for vagrant families turning up on their doorstep. That they did not always do so remains a scar on the history of the town.

Mary Summer and her son went into the workhouse in the autumn of 1840. The officious and sadistic Mr Salmon ran it. Mary's son misbehaved in some trivial manner and was punished by being locked in the mill-house for a day. Mary quite naturally told Mr Salmon that this was cruel. He simply shrugged and told her to get out. This she did, but she wasn't happy about it at all. A few hours later she was overheard complaining about the inhuman treatment of her son. Mr Salmon decided to make an example of her and maintain his regime of terror. Together with the porter, they grabbed her and dragged her up to the attic and threw her into the Black Hole. This was not much bigger than a broom cupboard and designed to punish and reform inmates who broke any of the myriad rules. Mary fought as best she could. She was suffering from consumption and half-starved. She received a deep bruise on her arm and ruptured a blood vessel in the fight, but into the hole she went.

Mary was kept in the dark cramped hole all of Friday night and Saturday, with no food or water at all. Mr Salmon relented on Saturday night and released her back to the ordinary ward of the workhouse, long after supper. Mary seemed weak on the Sunday; her consumption aggravated by her rough handling. She collapsed on Monday. A panicked Mr Salmon called a doctor on Tuesday, but Mary was now seriously ill. The doctor couldn't provide her with any real help and she died the next day.

Mr Salmon was now in an impossible situation. The doctor insisted on a post-mortem that revealed not only the injuries that she sustained as she was bundled into the Black Hole, but also that Mary had received no food for days. Mr Salmon at

There was nothing the doctor could do. Strand Magazine

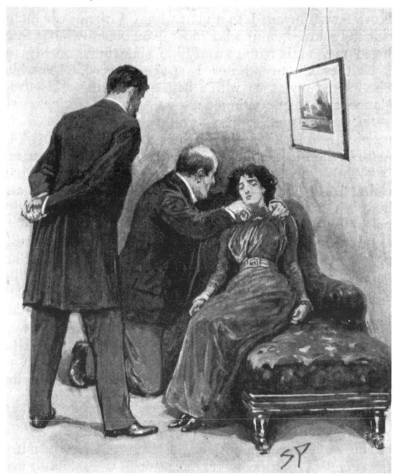

first swore that she had been given a bowl of gruel whilst she was incarcerated and then told him that she had even been given beef. 'I find this very strange considering the state of her stomach' the doctor told the inquest jury. Mary had been systematically starved and this had aggravated her consumption to the point where she died of congestion of the lungs. The jury wanted to find out more details of Mr Salmon's little empire.

They hit a wall of silence. The inmates of the workhouse were so terrified of Mr Salmon that they either refused to speak at all, or mumbled how nice the man was with frightened glances towards him. Only one witness spoke of the incident that provoked her punishment, Mr James told the jury how Mary had said to Salmon, 'he should have a hard pillow to sleep on for his cruelty to her son'.

Salmon justified his actions by accusing Mary of being brutal and violent. He even called her husband to testify to this effect. The jurors were not convinced. The establishment of Stratford closed ranks to support Salmon with surgeons and the trustees all testifying how wonderful the workhouse was. In a cutting remark the jury gave a verdict of death due to congestion of the lungs because they were unable to gather evidence to the contrary.

Soon enough Salmon was forced to resign and the management of the workhouse made slightly more open. Sadly Mary's death was not the end of the institutional neglect that paupers received in Stratford.

The Fisher family household collapsed over the summer of 1898. William and Mary Fisher lived at No 6 Henry's Row, Satchwell Street, Leamington. They had five children, the youngest of whom, Harriet, was only eighteen months old. William could only manage to find work collecting rags and bones, barely able to scratch a living. Their neighbour, Mrs Kirby, used to help feed little Harriet with bread and milk, but in the last weeks of May, Harriet was ill and she didn't see her. William and Mary were facing increasing amounts of debts.

The household finally collapsed on Sunday 5 June. The couple sold off what few bits of furniture they had left and set off on the road to seek work elsewhere. They walked all

Victorian workhouses offered an austere regime that split families apart in an attempt to make state aid as unattractive as possible. Indeed, many people preferred to starve rather than enter the forbidding institution. Strand Magazine

through the day, pushing the younger children in an old pram, and finally arrived at Stratford Workhouse at 6:00. William decided to press on towards Evesham where there was usually plenty of work in the fields. Mary and her children asked to see the nurse, as baby Harriet was not well.

The assistant Matron looked at the poorly baby and commented on her weak pulse. That was all the care she received that night. The following morning the wretched family were turned out of the workhouse at eight o'clock. They were given a small bottle of milk and some bread for the baby. They set off towards Alcester.

It was a long, hot and hard trek along the old turnpike road. Soon another vagrant, Margaret Glover, joined them. She was a widow with no home, and also heading to the workhouse at Alcester. The hours passed and Mary managed to get the baby to drink some milk, but could not get her to chew the bread. Harriet seemed reasonably well until half-past four, but then a terrible change came over her and she started to have convulsions.

They managed to make it to the Alcester Workhouse by six o'clock. There they received a much better welcome than at Stratford. Selina Burton, the assistant matron, was called immediately by one of the inmates, and came running, calling

The nineteenth century saw thousands of families wandering the roads in abject poverty. They moved from workhouse to workhouse, exploited and rejected by society. Charles Dickens exposed their dreadful conditions but it was not until the twentieth century that such total poverty was addressed successfully. Strand Magazine

for a nurse and the doctor. It was really too late now; Harriet was dying in Margaret's arms. The nurse tried giving her a little brandy and water but it was no help, Harriet died within ten minutes of their arrival.

A week later the coroner held an inquest into the circumstances of the tragic death. The various officers of the two workhouses tried shifting the blame elsewhere. Mary Fisher was accused of being a bad mother, William a neglectful father. Indeed their care may have been a contributory factor; Harriet weighed only ten pounds, just a third of the weight of a normal child at that age. The grinding poverty of her short life was the principal cause. Mary was in the Alcester Workhouse when Harriet was born, and the house they lived in at Leamington was described as a filthy and stinking hovel. In the final analysis, when the family needed desperately urgent help at Stratford Workhouse, they were ignored and sent on their way.

The blame ended up placed on the people who could least defend themselves. Mary and William Fisher were sentenced to six months' hard labour for child neglect.

CHAPTER 4

Hall End Farm
1808

A prodigious amount of blood and fragments of brain flowed from the victim's mouth.

Thomas Hardy's Wessex certainly doesn't have a monopoly when it comes to dysfunctional families. South Warwickshire has had its fair share too. Hall End Farm is situated in a sparsely populated area to the west of Henley in Arden, in 1808 the district was even more isolated and farming families and their communities of labourers turned in on themselves, hot housing their arguments and internecine squabbles.

Hall End was run by the patriarchal old Mr John Booth; a constable for the district and father of two sons and two daughters. John Booth junior took care of the management of the 250 acre farm, William Booth, his brother, now farmed 230 acres at Perry Barr, Ann Booth remained a spinster at Hall End and the other daughter had left to marry Mr Emery. In addition to the family there was a small group of labourers employed to do the arduous work. Thomas Gibbs at twenty-eight, was the most senior of these. There was John Allibone, a lad of just thirteen and Charlie Chamberlain, both of whom were ploughboys. Henry Lea was a more general-purpose labourer and John Pardy was the farm's waggoner, even though he was just eighteen. Inside the house Sarah Walford was the domestic servant and Ann French was another local woman who did out-work for the family, chiefly spinning flax. The farm was typical of its day, growing oats, barley and wheat as well as keeping a stock of cattle, pigs and goats. The main farmhouse was surrounded by a straggle of sheds, stables, hog sties, barns and, naturally, a kitchen garden and orchard. The farm was not merely self-sufficient but produced a healthy surplus of food that was needed by the rapidly expanding industrial towns of the Black Country. Farming was a profitable occupation and the basis of the English economy.

The Booth family was hardly the model of Georgian agriculture; indeed it is more reminiscent of the popular Victorian 'Dark Earth' novels like *Precious Bane*. The trouble seems to have started when the younger John Booth decided he must marry one of the servant girls. This was a thoroughly outrageous act in a society that was rigidly defined by class. The only possible excuse would have been that she was pregnant, but it seems that she wasn't. Love was not good enough for the rural gentry who had vast farms to consider in marriage settlements. Old Mr Booth was furious, William horrified and Ann disgusted. John and his new wife had to live in a small cottage about a mile away, his wife completely barred from ever visiting the farm.

The marriage, some time in the closing years of the eighteenth century, certainly got the local gossips going and the family was viewed with increasing suspicion. So too was their new labourer, Thomas Gibbs, and his wife. The young couple had moved into the farmhouse, Thomas as labourer and his wife as the domestic servant. Mr Booth decided that his son William, who was twenty-one, needed to be established in a farm of his own and he rented one for him at Perry Barr. This was a very generous move, 230 acres and substantial loans of cash to get it all going. William's brother, John, can not have been impressed; he was expected to live in a hovel and carry on the management of Hall End with just a subsistence wage. Thomas Gibbs had his eye on his job too, and had wheedled his way into the complete confidence of the rest of the family.

By 1805 it seems the village gossips had plenty to gloat over. One of Mr Booth's sons was rumoured to have attempted to poison the old man, and Thomas Gibbs was implicated in the plot. As the years passed this wasn't the only juicy bit of tittle-tattle. Soon the rumour was going the rounds that Miss Ann had been delivered of a bastard baby and had drowned it in the pond nearby. Thomas Gibbs' wife was suspected to be involved in the matter.

The constant open hostility between the two brothers was public knowledge. One day William had settled himself down with some friends in the *Nags Head* in Henley when Ann came into the pub. She asked him to come home with her but William refused, 'I should see that damned rogue Jack and if I did I should murder him and should think it no harm to do

There was a simmering feud between the brothers. Strand Magazine

so'. Ann assured him that his brother was not there and the local shoemaker, John Barnacle, remembered the vehemence of William's stark threat for some years.

John was fully aware of the loathing his brother held for him. A year later he was talking to Catherine Adcock, the butcher's wife in Henley. He told her that his father had ordered him to go to his brother's farm to help him out. He had refused to go, saying that he was afraid his brother would do him an injury.

February 1808 was yet another cold winter month. At the Perry Barr farm William was now an established member of the local gentry and had been appointed Overseer of the Poor, an important post in local government, and he was responsible for the distribution of poor relief to those in hardship. He had a reputation for great kindness and humanity in the execution of his duties. William had also married and now had a little daughter so he was a real member of the Perry Barr community. He wasn't afraid to work alongside his own farm labourers and earned their respect in the process. It had its drawbacks though, on 16 February he was helping his men, Mark Layton, William Thorpe and John Burton kill a pig. They heaved it up to bleed it and the blood spilt all over his waistcoat and new breeches. He muttered about spoiling his breeches and his neighbour, Sarah Smith, said 'Sir, I think you have spoiled your waistcoat too, you have bloodied it as well'. William said he wasn't too upset about the waistcoat, it was old and the buttons were gone. He would probably never wear it again.

A couple of days later, on Thursday 18 February William took his wife and daughter down to Hall End Farm to stay a few days. He was on good terms with his father and sister even if not quite so friendly with his brother. On the Friday morning the work of the farm continued its eternal cycle.

John Pardy went into the stable at first light to get the three heavy horses into their gear to be ready for ploughing if the weather warmed. In the long stable the horses had stalls along one side, and at the far end was a pitch door, a half height door used for throwing out the stable litter and dung. Charles Chamberlain came in and opened it up when he mucked out the horses. He left it open when he was called to help with moving an oat rick. The horses were left in their gear and haltered just in case the weather lifted enough to continue the ploughing. In every farm across the land the horses were the first to be looked after, they provided all the strength needed to work the land, just like tractors today. The big difference is that tractors don't have personalities. Of the three heavy horses John Pardy cared for, the one in the stall by the door was a bad tempered vicious mare with a tendency to kick. The village blacksmith, William Godwin, knew all about her little ways. She kicked him whenever she got the chance. One time she had kicked his lad, Francis Bolt, so hard that he flew through the air and landed some way off, when he picked him up the poor boy was unable to speak for ages.

The main task for the day was moving an oat rick closer to the stables. John Pardy hitched up a couple of other horses to the wagon and together with Henry Lee, John Allibone and Thomas Gibbs set to. The work was long and laborious, loading the straw onto the wagon, hauling it from the rick yard, through the fold yard and then stacking it under the elm trees as young Master John had instructed them. John Allibone probably had the most fun as he rode on top of the wobbling load. Time and again they ferried loads across the farm.

William grabbed a bite of lunch at noon, but the men's lunch was delayed until about two-thirty. Sarah Walford had got it all ready for the men but they were late coming in. This was because William had come out to them and enquired why they were not stacking the straw by the barn as his father had instructed. John Pardy was not impressed after carting the stuff about all morning and told him that Master John had told them where to put it. Old Mr Booth and John came into the yard and they argued about it for a while, then Mr Booth went back to the house and John went to the stables. The horses had been left in their gear far too long and there wouldn't be enough time left now to get any worthwhile ploughing done before dark. William stayed by the wagon a while longer.

Sarah Walford stormed out of the kitchen and demanded to know if they meant to have any dinner at all today. William went up to the house and into the main kitchen. Thomas and Henry tidied up a bit before going to the servant's kitchen. There they met Ann French. She had brought some spinning up to the farm for Ann Booth. It wasn't a very lucrative job, but it was something she could do from home to earn a little extra money. Ann French sat down to eat some bread and cheese that Miss Booth gave her, and swap tips about growing beans with old Mr Booth who sat smoking his pipe.

Ann French got up out of her chair so that Thomas Gibbs could sit down. As she did so she noticed William leave the main kitchen. Ann Booth asked her if she could spin a bag of clearings for her. These were the refuse left from the flax crop and could only be used for common sheeting. Henry Lee said he would drop them round to her house that evening after work. Ann French left the kitchen and walked along the garden path, as she did so she noticed William walking towards the stables.

Sarah Walford, despairing about the lateness of the lunch, went upstairs to get on with making the beds. She crossed the bedroom and looked out of the open window. There she saw Ann French walking off towards the orchard. Sarah finished off the bed and returned to the window. It gave her an unparalleled view of the yards and stables. She saw Miss Booth go to the garden gate and call 'John'. On getting no response she went over to the orchard and called again several times. Still getting no response she walked back down the side of the cowshed. Across the yard, invisible to Ann, William Booth appeared from the fold yard and walked towards the garden. He reached the privy and saw his daughter there. He asked her where her mother was and she told him she was in the house. He hurried off to the house.

Out in the yard John Allibone and Charles Chamberlain were still by the wagon. John noticed Miss Ann come into the cow yard, and she called across to him to come and help her fetch a basket. They got as far as the shed when Ann turned her head and noticed something in the stable. She told John she thought she saw someone lying down. She then went to the house while John went to investigate.

What John found was really not suitable for a thirteen-year-old lad.

'Master John! Master John!' he cried as he found his master lying in the stable dirt, his face all covered in blood and his hat battered and dented. There was no reply. He lay on his left side, his head beside the standing post. A few feet away stood the vicious mare; her leather harness lay on top of Master John. John Allibone stood up and went outside to call for help; Charles Chamberlain went in and again tried to wake the fallen man by calling his name. Pardy held John Booth's hand and called his name. He took up the harness gear and hung it up in its proper place.

Thomas Gibbs was still in the servants' kitchen when Ann Booth came in suddenly and shouted, 'Lord have mercy on me, my brother is very much hurt, he is all over blood'. Thomas Gibbs rushed to the stable. As he went he distinctly heard William Booth beside the pigsties saying 'What a terrible noise these pigs are making, I will let them out'. Who he was talking to Thomas could not make out.

Thomas got to the stable and tried to see what was the matter. John Booth had his mouth full of blood, so Thomas put his fingers in to try and get his airway open. He flicked the blood off his fingers onto the floor and then heaved the apparently unconscious body upright. In doing so his bloody hand left a red imprint on the standing post. Realising the damage was to John's head he tried to take off his hat. It was jammed on tight and took an effort to remove. The hat was full of blood and very dented. As Thomas dragged the body towards the door for some air William Booth arrived.

'Lord have mercy on me,' William cried.

Thomas ordered the lads to get a chair with arms so that they could carry John to the house and William told him to take his horse and ride for the surgeon. John was carried up to the kitchen and sat in front of the fire. It was just about three o'clock.

It didn't take long for the news to get out. Somebody alerted John Tarleton at the neighbouring farm, some 500 yards away, within a few minutes. He got to Hall End shortly after three and went to see old Mr Booth. Mr Booth was in a quandary; he was the constable but as the accident was on his farm he couldn't very well police himself. John Tarleton would simply have to act as a special constable for the time being. It seemed pretty straightforward, the blasted mare had done what she liked doing best, kicking hell out of anyone in range. In this case it had resulted in the death of John Booth. Such incidents were all too common.

Mr Burman, the surgeon from Henley, arrived at around 4:15, quickly followed by another, Thomas Owen Jones. It seems that William Booth had become impatient with the speed Thomas Gibbs was making on his old nag, and sent someone else as well, on a faster horse. The result was two surgeons arriving virtually together. The various lads of the farm were finally allowed to get their lunch in the servants' kitchen whilst the surgeons laid the corpse of John Booth on the main kitchen table. Hopefully they closed the adjoining door.

The surgeons realised the massive extent of the head injuries since when they turned the body over, a prodigious amount of blood and fragments of brain flowed from the victim's mouth. They washed and gently cut off John's hair to reveal the injuries. They were horrified to discover wounds that could never have been inflicted by a horse's hoof. John had six injuries, three on the right, two on the left and one on the back. The wounds would have all been horizontal when the victim was standing upright. They were all inflicted with a straight edged, though blunt, instrument. There was virtually no bruising or laceration. No horseshoe could possibly wound like that; the two surgeons rushed out to the stable.

John Allibone had finished his meal and been sent back out to the stable to do his usual chores. He took a spade from its normal place and started scraping up the horse dung from the floor and chucking it through the open pitch hole. After a few minutes John Tarleton and the two surgeons came in, took one look at the spade and took it off him. They examined it closely and found blood soaked into the dirt as well as a patch of wet blood by the left tread. John Allibone assured them that he had only used it to scrape up a little of the blood stained litter. It looked to them as though they were holding the murder weapon. This was no ordinary agricultural accident.

John Tarleton was probably not the Georgian equivalent of Sherlock Holmes, although he was an astute businessman and farmer. He instructed John Pardy to bring the mare out of the stable and he inspected her hind hooves, taking care not to get a kicking himself. The left hoof was missing a shoe and the right one was very worn and polished. The horse had very long hair on its legs and he examined this minutely for traces of blood. He found none at all. The following day when he discovered William Booth intended to return to Perry Barr, he insisted that he return on Monday for the inquest. He also took possession of the spade and hat. He also made a note of what William Booth was wearing, and instructed the blacksmith to remove the worn shoe from the vicious mare.

On Monday he received the horseshoe, and instructed Robert Ashfield, the Stratford Constable, to go up to Perry Barr to find William's waistcoat. William had turned up for the preliminary inquest wearing fresh clothes, in particular a nice clean light coloured coat. The old waistcoat had blood on it, which seemed to confirm John Tarleton's suspicions. By the end of the week William was under arrest for the murder of his brother. The village gossip had been of such a damning nature that no one was surprised at a murder as well as the other dark goings on at Hall End Farm.

The case was brought before Warwick assizes on 8 April. The scurrilous gossip that fascinated the village had now reached most of the county and someone had published a vitriolic pamphlet suggesting William was guilty. It was looking very bleak for William. The surgeons were adamant that the wounds to John's head were inflicted by the spade and not by the horse. Ann French swore she had seen William going towards the stable and then there was the blood on his waistcoat. It seemed to make a virtually watertight prosecution case. Warwick Assizes was packed with spectators and for ten hours the jury listened to the evidence and defence. William had little in the way of a defence; he called witnesses to show that the bloodstains on his waistcoat were from the pig he had been slaughtering on the Tuesday. His defence lawyers managed to tangle up the surgeon Thomas Owen Jones; it turned out that he had never dealt with injuries inflicted by a horse before. Ann French admitted that she hadn't seen William for some years, and hadn't clearly seen the face of the person in the dark blue coat going towards the stables. A couple of other witnesses described how they had dealings with the vicious mare, and also how a hat could remain undamaged even though their scalp had been cut by a fall against something hard. The majority of his witnesses were character references from the farmers and neighbours of Perry Barr, all of whom said how he had proved himself to be a kind and humane man, a good Overseer of the Poor and an upright member of society.

The judge, the Honourable Sir George Wood, summed up the case at length. He went through the prosecution evidence showing how it failed to prove that William was actually in the stable. Although the surgeons had seemed convinced that the mare had not inflicted the fatal wounds, the judge was not. He stressed that it was a most unusual time to attempt to murder someone, when all the family and staff were about. He concluded with a stern warning to the jury that it is always better that twenty guilty men go free rather than one innocent man be executed. The jury needed only twenty minutes to conclude that William was not guilty.

The question still remains, did the mare kick John Booth to death, or did his brother settle an old score and ensure his inheritance with a spade and some direct action? Once the case was concluded, Hall End settled back into its comfortable obscurity and no more questions were asked.

Four years passed. Old Mr Booth died and William inherited the farm. No doubt the gossips kept an eye on the farm. They were not to be disappointed. Staffordshire constables were investigating a counterfeiting gang who were striking coins made from the melted down handles of coffins. Fake coins were circulating in vast quantities because of the economic mess of the Napoleonic Wars. Large businesses were forced to pay their workers in tokens because all the copper was being used to make cannons and pennies were as rare as hens' teeth. Base metal fakes weren't too difficult to strike and a small press could easily be hidden in an attic.

The Staffordshire constables raided William Booth's farm in Perry Barr. A thorough search revealed a coining press in the attic and William Booth was arrested as the ringleader of the gang. This time he was found guilty when the case came before the assizes. No amount of references could help him this time. Counterfeiting was a capital offence and he was sentenced to death.

Justice in 1812 involved an awful lot of hanging. By the time William was due for the long drop, they had worn out their old scaffold and had to build a brand new one. William was the first to try it out. The hangman stood him on the trapdoor, blindfolded him, pinioned his arms behind his back and carefully arranged the noose around his neck. It was a matter of pride for executioners to get the noose just right. Unfortunately this chap spent so much time getting the noose right, he had quite forgotten the other end of the rope. A roll of the drums, the lever pulled, the trap fell, William Booth dropped, and so did the rope. Booth hit the floor twelve feet below with a sickening thud. The executioner had to drag the semiconscious man back up, stand him on the trap and try again. This time he made sure the rope was tied to the scaffold. Another roll of the drums, the lever pulled … and nothing. The trap door jammed. Quite what William Booth was making of all this remains a mystery. The crowds were getting restless whilst the executioner messed about with the trap door. One last time the drums rolled, the lever pulled, and this time it was the end of William Booth.

CHAPTER 5

The Heytrey Children
1819
Ann followed the spots of blood across the hall and up the stairs...

On Ladyday 1818 Ann Heytrey started work as a servant for the Dormer family at the Dial House in the parish of Ashow, just north of Warwick. Joseph and Sarah Dormer had six children and another three servants, so Ann had plenty of work to do in the kitchen.

Dial House is situated on the outskirts of the village of Ashow between Warwick and Kenilworth. It was the scene of a violent and sudden murder that is still part of the local folklore. The author

Ann was just twenty. She had been brought up in the village of Charlecote, between Stratford and Wellesbourne. Her father had spent his life as an agricultural labourer but had died a few years earlier, leaving Ann and her brother Thomas to be brought up by their mother, in very straightened circumstances. Life in rural England during the Napoleonic Wars was difficult, to say the least. There was widespread poverty and even though many men had gone to fight the French farm wages remained low. When the wars ended in 1815, the returning soldiers flooded the labour market and depressed wages still further. The gentlemen farmers of the time were building massive farm holdings and finishing off the enclosure of common lands so that the ordinary labourers could no longer collect firewood or the wild fruits. The economy was a shambles after the wars, with nearly as many forged notes in circulation as real ones. Copper coins were so rare that many labourers could only be paid when their wages reached a sum that could be paid in silver. A loaf of bread cost a day's wages.

In the spring of 1819 Ann Heytrey attempted to take away some notes from the Dial House. Her brother, Thomas, had already gained a reputation as a crook and could probably have passed them off amongst his underworld contacts. This was not to be as Ann was caught before the notes could be spirited away. This was a capital offence, and Ann would have been dragged on a hurdle through the streets of Warwick before being hanged. Justice in Georgian England was stern and severe, specifically intended to ensure that social order was maintained, if not by consent, then absolute terror. Public execution was the sentence for many offences; the alternative was transportation to the newly expanding colonies.

Ann was extremely fortunate that Sarah Dormer spoke up for her at her trial and the charges were laid aside. In a very real sense Ann Heytrey owed her mistress her life. It was a debt that she seemed to take seriously, later remarking:

I liked my mistress so much I would have got up at any hour of the night to serve her.

Ann was now twenty-one. She was slightly shorter than average but a stoutly-built girl with striking dark brown hair and eyes. Her face was described as 'comely' although not beautiful and her hands had already been coarsened by the long hours of toil in the kitchen and laundry of the Dial House. The household seemed to function in a perfectly normal manner, Mr Joseph Dormer engaged in business and farming, whilst Sarah managed the household. Their six children ranged from about five to seventeen. Ann tended the kitchen and laundry whilst Richard Smith, John Branstone and J. Barnacle looked after the carts, wagons and grounds.

Sunday 29 August 1819 was a special day for the village. It was the parish Wake, a little festival of thanksgiving. Mr Joseph Dormer invited some of his colleagues to attend the festivities. The two Mr Brays of Coventry and Mr Dormer went to see the wake whilst Mrs Dormer stayed in the house arranging lunch for Mr Thomas Harris and Mr William Hinde.

After lunch the group spent the afternoon drinking tea and chatting until about six o'clock. It was a fine evening and the two gentlemen decided to take a walk to Mr Aldridge's house at Thickthorn, taking the children with them. Sarah stayed in the house with Ann Heytrey. All the other servants had gone to the wake.

It was the wake, and the children of the area were wandering about all over the place. Two of them appeared at the back door and Sarah gave them each a glass of wine and some cucumbers to take home with them. The children left by the front door. Sarah and Ann went out into the kitchen garden and picked some more cucumbers for supper. They returned to the house and Sarah went into the best kitchen. She put on her spectacles and sat down to read a book. Out in the road Miss E Jaggard and her friends were walking back to her house, 'The Forge'. She saw Sarah sitting by the window. Suddenly she noticed Ann, wearing a deep red dress with a coarse apron, walk out into the road, look down it towards the village, and then walk back into the house.

Sarah Dormer was sitting quietly reading her book in the sunny window. Her wealthy husband and his guests were enjoying the wake, her children and the other guests taking a pleasant stroll and her maidservant was busy chopping up onions and cucumbers in the scullery. Her privileged and tranquil life was about to be shattered.

Ann Heytrey was halfway through chopping up the onions when a thought suddenly occurred to her. She must kill her mistress. She put down the knife and walked into the kitchen. Sarah must have looked up at her presence. Ann smashed her fist full into her mouth so hard that it knocked out two of her front teeth and flung her to the floor. She lay there for a few seconds as Ann stood above her. Ann kicked and punched her again. Whimpering in pain and fear she scrabbled up and ran into the hall and up the stairs. Ann returned to the scullery and picked up the kitchen knife. Sarah was now cowering in her bedroom. Ann followed the spots of blood across the hall and up the stairs, cornering Sarah in her bedroom. Sarah attempted to fend off the furious blows of the knife, and had her hands cut to the bone. She must have dropped to her knees. Ann grabbed her hair and face and then hacked at her throat, first cutting across her jaw and then repeatedly slashing the blade through her windpipe until the steel reached her spine. Sarah's blood poured from the wound onto Ann's apron and red dress, she fell backwards to the floor, her life ebbing away with each weakening spurt. Ann took a black cap and placed it under her shoulder, placed the knife carefully beside her arm and went downstairs.

Quite methodically Ann now removed the blood-steeped apron and took it out to the washing tub and put it in to soak. She went back into the house and made a desultory effort to clean up the spots of blood in the hall. She took the bloodied towel out to the tub as well. Standing alone in the hall in the now silent house, the strange mood that had come over Ann suddenly left her. The homicidal fury subsided as quickly as it came, leaving Ann confused and shivering in fright.

The children arrived back from their walk at ten past seven, just a few moments later. Elizabeth opened the back door and found Ann standing in the passageway. She was shaking and sweating heavily. She appeared dazed and distressed and went out of the back door without a word. Elizabeth, Joseph, Mary and Harriett stood in the hall wondering what on earth was

the matter with her. Ann came back in and Elizabeth asked her
if anyone had come to the house. Ann said that nobody had,
but seemed completely confused. Elizabeth asked where her
mother was and Ann told the seventeen-year-old that she had
gone towards Ashow. Joseph now pointed to the drops of
blood on the floor and Elizabeth asked her,

Nancy, what is this?
Oh, nothing.

Elizabeth told her to get a mop and clear it up. Her younger
sister Harriett called out for her mother and asked Ann where
she was. This time Ann said that she was in the garden picking
cucumbers. It was all very odd. Elizabeth and Mary went
upstairs to their rooms. Elizabeth noticed that the door to her
mother's room on the left of the landing was closed. She went
into her room opposite. Mary, being only fourteen, really
wanted to see her mother and tell her about the wake. She
opened the bedroom door.
　　Her screams rang out through the house:

Murder! My mother is murdered!

Out in the road a surgeon by the name of Bodington heard the
shrieks and spurred his horse right across the garden to the
front door. Downstairs Joseph raced out to the woodshed and
grabbed the nearest weapon he could find, a fork, and ran up
the stairs. Ann Heytrey followed him. They stood staring at the
ruined body of Sarah Dormer weltering in a pool of blood.
　　Joseph grabbed Ann's hand and dragged her downstairs and
out into the yard. He slapped her hard across the face.

*You have no occasion to pull me, I'll go where you have a mind
to take me,*

she muttered.
　　Joseph dragged her into the road and shouted:

You have killed my mother!

Ann just shrugged and made no reply.

In the house Mr Bodington examined Sarah Dormer; she was definitely dead. He decided to seal up the room and call the constable. Word was spreading rapidly around the district. Samuel Turner had taken charge of Ann from the distraught Joseph. He held her until Thomas Bellerby, the constable from Kenilworth arrived at half-past eight. He asked Ann if she was the servant who had killed her mistress.

'They say so, but I am not.' The constable was not convinced; her hands were covered in blood. He asked her if the apron she had on was the one she was wearing earlier. 'No' she said it was not, and the other apron was hanging on the woodshed door. Thomas Bellerby took her away to gaol.

The following day Mr Bodington and another surgeon, Mr Hiron, came back to conduct a proper autopsy. Thomas Bellerby came back to examine the scene as well. He found the bloodstained apron and towel and decided it would be wise to interview Ann's brother, Thomas. There seemed to be no logical motive for the murder other than robbery, and Thomas had a reputation in that department. He was arrested that afternoon.

It was the arrest of her brother that finally brought Ann out of her sullen silence. Constable Bellerby told her that he had been taken into custody and she replied,

What a thing it is to bring my friends into trouble. Neither my brother nor no other man had to do with the murder.
If you say that, you know who did it.

Ann went on to describe how she suddenly felt compelled to kill her mistress, the assault in the kitchen and the terrible violence in the bedroom. Thomas Bellerby was aghast at her words,

Did she make resistance?
Very little.
Did she cry out?
No.
Why did you not run away?

I was so confused I did not know what to do.
Had your mistress done or said something in the course of the day
to offend you?
She had never given me an angry word.

Ann finally broke down in tears and sobbed that she liked her mistress so much that she would have done anything for her. She could not explain the strange and sudden compulsion that had made her kill her.

At the Lent assizes the following spring Ann Heytrey was found guilty of petty treason and sentenced to death. On 10 April, a few days before her execution she wrote the following letter to Elizabeth Dormer:

Dear Miss Dolmar,

I take the liberty of addressing you with this epistle for the last time and I am heartily sorry for the sorrowful misfortune as has happened which I hope the Lord in his mercies will forgive me and I was very sorry to see you look so bad. I did not know you when you was called up. I hope you will forgive me for what I have done as my life will pay for the unfortunate deed. Oh may the Almighty be your comfort and may he pardon me my sins. Miss Dolmar I ask your forgiveness and the family's at large…

Elizabeth Dormer had indeed changed. It is no wonder Ann failed to recognise her in the crowded courtroom. Harriett and Mary had spent most of their time in court sobbing, but Elizabeth had found the strength of character to stand upright and give her evidence in a clear bold manner that earned the respect of everyone who heard her.

On Wednesday 12 April Ann Heytrey was bound to a hurdle outside Warwick Gaol and dragged to the scaffold. Right up to the last moment she insisted that the killing was because of that strange compulsion and that she had no other motive. She begged forgiveness once again, and the trap fell. An hour later her body was cut down and conveyed to the surgeon, Mr Bodington, at Kenilworth for dissection. Perhaps he hoped to find the reason for this apparently inexplicable murder in his studies of anatomy.

Thomas Heytrey lodged in this cottage before he was arrested. Originally the building was two separate farm workers' cottages. The author

Thomas Heytrey may well have been in the vast crowd that came to Warwick to see the execution of his sister. He had now left home and was living in lodgings at Pimlico, a tiny hamlet near Loxley. It was only a couple of hours walk to the town.

Thomas was mixing with some very dubious characters indeed. There were plenty about. Agricultural wages were still declining and the civil unrest that was to lead to the Captain Swing Riots was already starting. Ann Heytrey's trial had been interrupted when the judge announced that there had been bloodshed in a fight between civilians and the military in Scotland. The workers of Clydeside had rebelled against their appalling conditions. Life in rural Warwickshire was not much better; there were footpads and gangs roaming the turnpikes looking for easy pickings.

Through the summer of 1820 several people were attacked and robbed on the roads around Stratford. The magistrates believed it to be the work of at least one gang, possibly more. The traffic on the turnpike roads consisted of goods wagons and coaches, which were usually safe because of the numbers of people, gentlemen on horseback, who could usually canter away from trouble, and pedestrians, who frequently didn't have enough money to be worth robbing anyway. For the highway robbers it was a bit of a thin time of it; they needed something to get at the rich gentlemen on their high horses.

Thomas Heytrey was working as a blacksmith and in the autumn of that year met a trio of villains who were living in the row of small dwellings on the Banbury Road just outside the town, called Waterloo Cottages. Nathaniel Quiney and Henry Adams were already old hands at mugging people on the turnpikes. A blacksmith, Samuel Sidney, moved into the row of cottages and added an extra element of viciousness to their activities. Quiney and Adams tended to avoid hurting their victims. They simply wanted the money to help maintain their

Samuel Sidney, Nathaniel Quiney and Henry Adams lived in this row of cottages. Quiney and Adams both had large families to support on very meagre earnings. The cottages are now hidden by staggeringly inappropriate development on the Banbury Road. The author

large families. Quiney had seven children and Adams six. Adams' wife was expecting their next child. Both men had to find the money to feed all these children on their small earnings as labourers looking after horses. Samuel Sidney was married, but had no children. He had a violent streak in his personality and was not satisfied with simply stealing enough to get by on. He pestered and bullied the other two to commit more and more robberies. It seems that Sidney was the most ambitious and intelligent of them all. He was the only one capable of writing and it may well have been him who came up with the idea of getting mounted gentlemen off their horses.

The problem of attacking mounted people was simply one of height. You got a face full of riding boot as like as not. If you had some kind of hook to pull the rider off, then matters would be much simpler. Quiney managed to find an old scythe back and persuaded a blacksmith's apprentice, Richard Cox, to fashion a socket for it. He then fixed a long handle onto the curved hook.

Thomas Heytrey worked at numerous farms with his trade of blacksmith. He discovered that Mr Parker, the bailiff for Mr Bradley, the farmer at Alveston Crofts, would be coming back from market in Warwick on the evening of Saturday 4 November. Mr Parker would be carrying a substantial quantity of cash and be on horseback. What better opportunity would the gang have to try out their new weapon?

During the week Quiney and Adams, probably Sidney as well, tried a few robberies on the Shipston and Warwick Roads, but they failed to get enough booty to make it worthwhile. Saturday night was to be the big one.

Thomas Heytrey and Samuel Sidney arranged to meet on the turnpike road between Stratford and Wellesbourne just after dark. Adams and Quiney were to join up with them a little later. Thomas came directly from his work at the Bradley's farm. He was wearing a light-coloured fustian smock as a result. Sidney, Adams and Quiney wore heavy dark great-coats and had blacked their faces so as to conceal their identities. Sidney carried a four-foot long stick that had a massive knot, the size of two fists, on its end. Quiney had his new hook on a six-foot pole, and Adams had a nasty contraption. It was apparently an ordinary stick with a skittle-shaped handle. The handle could be pulled off and fixed on sideways like a long mallet.

As the four villains set off the fog closed in. It was a foul night, perfectly suited to their purpose. They met up near the turnpike gate by Halfords Barn just beyond Tiddington and started walking towards Wellesbourne. Adams and Quiney walked ahead of the other two. There were few others on the road. Someone they took to be a miller walked past them and they bade him goodnight. A jig rattled past, but they let it pass unmolested. Richard Vincent and his son wandered by. The night was so dark and foggy that they only recognised him by his voice. They reached Littleham Bridge at about eight o'clock. In the thick foggy darkness they waited in silence. There seemed to be no more travellers on the road. At nine they finally heard the distant sound of hooves. Heytrey called out that it must be Parker and he dived behind the hedge. He was both visible and recognisable. The three others took their places at the sides of the bridge.

William Hiron was probably in a cheerful mood as he trotted along the turnpike. He had come back home to stay

It is easy to miss this small bridge just beyond Alveston today as you whiz past in a car, but once it was the scene of a horrific attack on an innocent man. The author

with his mother in Alveston. Normally he lived in London but he retained his right to vote in the Warwickshire County elections. He had gone to Warwick that day to go see his brother Henry and cast his vote in the election held that day. Elections in those days were rather different to those of today. Very few people were allowed to vote for one thing; it was anything but secret, and the candidates wooed the voters by the simple expedient of buying them lots of beer. William had spent a fair part of the day in the *Bowling Green* pub and then cast his vote for Mr Lawley. He set off from the pub at about eight and by nine had reached Littleham Bridge.

Henry Adams jumped out into the road and used the hook to pull William off his horse. He landed heavily on the road but managed to jump up straight away. Sidney and Quiney went up to him, Sidney striking him twice with his bludgeon and Quiney went at him from behind, hitting him across the shoulders with his stick.

William struggled to stay upright. He spread his arms and said they could take his money and he would forgive them. Sidney merely hit him again and again until he collapsed to the ground. Henry Adams and Nathaniel Quiney rifled through William's pockets, pulling out a notecase from his left coat pocket and some loose change from the other. Sidney kept hitting him.

Damn it, don't hurt him, we don't want any more of him.

Henry was getting alarmed at Sidney's violence.

Henry decided they had got everything and said they should get away. He dragged William Hiron out of the centre of the road so that any passing carriages wouldn't run him over. As they walked away they noticed William attempt to sit up and he groaned,

By Heavens, don't hurt me anymore.

Samuel Sidney walked back. Through the thick fog they heard the sound of two heavy, hard blows, but couldn't see what was happening. Sidney rejoined them a few seconds later.

Did you hit him on the boots? asked Henry, *It rattled so.*
No, I hit him on the head.
Sam, what a fool you be. I don't wish to hurt any man in the world.

The robbery complete, the four of them vanished into the fog to make their separate ways home across the fields. Thomas Heytrey got back to his lodgings with Ann Mercer at Pimlico at half-nine. The rest got to Waterloo Cottages half an hour later. They gathered in Quiney's house to see what they had managed to steal and how to share it out. Quiney had even stolen Mr Hiron's hat.

William Hiron regained consciousness somewhat later. Battered and bleeding heavily from several severe head wounds, he was partially paralysed down his right side. He was alone on the road in the cold and in pitch, foggy darkness. His horse had bolted and he knew only that he must somehow get home. There would be no rescuers this late on a little country lane. Groaning in agony he staggered to his feet and, struggling to maintain his balance, he started off towards the warmth and safety of his family home. He only needed to walk about half a mile and take the first turn on the right. In his blaze of pain he didn't realise he was going in entirely the wrong direction, further in to the cold empty night.

The alarm was raised early on Sunday morning when William's horse was found standing patiently outside its stable; of William there seemed to be no sign.

Elizabeth Spiers set off from her home in Charlecote towards Hunscott on Sunday morning. She had crossed the turnpike road and gone about forty yards further when she saw a man lying on his back in the ditch.

Lord have mercy on me. How came you here in this state?

William could not reply. He was so terribly wounded and now suffering from hypothermia. He had walked half a mile and turned right, and collapsed, not into his family home, but a ditch in the middle of nowhere. Elizabeth dragged him out and sat him on the verge. Luckily George Busby came along the road, and realising the gravity of the situation raced around to Mr Lucas's farm to get a horse and cart. Elizabeth and George managed to lift William into the back and they set off towards Stratford to get to a doctor. James Wallington, the farmer at Charlecote, overtook them and recognising William, got into the cart beside him and directed them to William's home.

William Sutton, the groom for Sir Gray Skipwith, when he passed over Littleham Bridge early that morning, noticed a bunch of keys, broken brace buckles, shreds of clothing and, more ominously, a large pool of blood. He picked up the keys to take back to his master. Not long after Thomas Nicholls, the shoemaker from Alveston, came by. He stopped at the sight of blood and picked up a riding stick that was lying nearby. Standing there in puzzlement, Henry Hiron arrived on his horse. He had been alarmed at the arrival of his brother's horse and set out to search for him. He recognised the riding stick; it was his own.

William was brought into the house and James Wallington carried him up to his bedroom. Mary Alridge helped James undress and wash him. William was barely conscious and managed to rally slightly as they warmed him up, he managed a hoarse, weak whisper:

Three villains...

and he fell back exhausted.

Thomas Heytrey and the three villains were arguing about how to divide their spoils. Thomas had made his way to Quiney's house on Sunday morning. The gang sat in the hovel at the back of Waterloo Cottages. Quiney had shoved his iron hook into the thatch to conceal it. They gloated over their haul. It consisted of a few silver coins and a notebook containing three one pound notes. They exchanged coins and the notes until they all felt they had a fair share. The pound notes were going to be a problem. Each note was quite distinctive, one was a Bank of England note, easy enough to exchange; one was from the Buckingham Bank and the other from Leighton Buzzard, both of these were legal tender but extremely rare and distinctive in Stratford. They represented a small fortune to the men who were earning about two shillings a week. Henry Adams hid the Leighton Buzzard note away in the webbing of his bedside chair, Heytrey got the Buckingham note and Sidney the Bank of England one. They decided to keep the notes hidden until the matter had been forgotten.

William Hiron lingered, just about able to recognise his relatives, until midnight on Tuesday. His wounds were incapable of being treated. There were four massive gashes in his skull, one of which went right through to his brain. He shook his head and tried to talk but no one could make out what he meant. He died without saying another word. The hunt was now on for murderers not just highwaymen.

Henry Hiron and Mr Greenway, William's executors, offered a reward of two hundred guineas for information leading to the capture of the rogues. John Ashfield, one of the Stratford constables, had a fairly good idea of where to start looking. On Thursday he made his way to Mr Bradley's farm to interview Thomas Heytrey. He caught him coming out of the house and immediately charged him with the murder. Thomas naturally denied it, but he was not an accomplished liar. He could give no satisfactory answer as to his whereabouts on the fatal Saturday night. He became muddled up, saying first that he had heard of the murder at work, and then at his lodgings.

In the afternoon John Ashfield put on the pressure. Mr Greenway sat at the desk in the parlour and pretended to write down everything that was said. Greenway put down a wad of £200 and suggested that it could be his if he revealed the names of the other men. He may even get a free pardon. Thomas Heytrey fell for the ploy and told them the whole sorry story. He was instantly arrested and taken to Stratford. The money went back into Greenway's pocket.

Instructions were sent out to apprehend Sidney, Adams and Quiney while John Ashfield went to search Heytrey's lodgings. Ann Mercer confirmed that Heytrey had not returned until after nine on the Saturday, and she showed him a box belonging to Thomas. In it he found several pound notes, a small fortune for an apparently penniless blacksmith. John

The Falcon Inn *was the home of the town constable. The highwaymen were plied with strong ale and offered vast amounts of cash until they confessed. Once the confessions were obtained, they were doomed.* The author

Ashfield returned to Stratford to find all the gang locked up in his house.

The following morning they were allowed some time to converse before being interviewed by the magistrate. It was a simple enough plan to get at the truth. The interview was to take place in the *Falcon Inn*, and by the time they got to see the magistrate, each of them had been given ten horns of ale. They were drunk. Quiney was in tears and Adams full of remorse, only Sidney retained his composure. Mr Greenway with his large wad of money attended the coroner, Mr Hunt, once again. It may have been highly irregular, but the ruse succeeded in getting four detailed and signed confessions. The gang was sent to Warwick Gaol to await the Lent Assizes.

The trial was held on 12 April 1821. It didn't take very long. The men tried to explain that their confessions were extracted from them by bribery when they had been induced to become drunk. Mr Hunt and Mr Greenway naturally denied this and stated the men were all quite sober when they signed their confessions. The judge had no qualms about sentencing them all to death. Heytrey tried to say that he was innocent of the murder because he was hiding behind the bridge, but the judge dismissed this instantly. They had all conspired together to attack the man, and they all therefore shared the consequences.

Two days later they were dragged to the scaffold. Adams was in a pitiful state, whilst he had been in the gaol his wife had died giving birth to his seventh child. Now all his children were to be orphaned. Quiney, too, was broken with grief. Heytrey seemed resigned to his ghastly fate: to die on the same scaffold as his sister had done the previous year. Samuel Sidney seemed entirely unaffected by the process.

The prayers were said and the trap fell. Quiney and Adams died quickly; Sidney struggled and jerked about for what seemed like an eternity. Heytrey barely struggled at all, but lived the longest of any of them. Their bodies were cut down and sent away to be dissected by various Warwickshire surgeons. It was the end of a vicious gang of footpads that had preyed on the people of Stratford.

CHAPTER 6

Bare Knuckle Fighting
1833
*They dragged him back to his house and called
the local surgeon.*

The ability to fight one's way out of poverty with just bare fists has always been an option. In 1833 there were often prizefights with rewards of hundreds of pounds, occasionally even a thousand. For many labourers victory in a fight could bring wealth and status unobtainable in any other way. To start on this rather perilous route to fortune first you needed a reputation as a good fighter.

On 9 September 1833 William York, George Morris and Isaac Barnett were drinking the afternoon away in the *Anchor* at the bottom of Bridge Street. The pub had managed to get itself a fairly rough reputation as the haunt of the dockers working on the boats and tram wagons. The boatmen were paid low wages for the back-breaking work of unloading coal and corn from the boats. The meagre wages tended to be supplemented with a little petty pilfering of the cargoes. William York was a strong man with a reputation as a reasonable fighter. William Jackson, another labourer with a similar reputation, walked into the pub around 4:30. It wasn't long before York challenged Jackson to a fight.

Jackson really just wanted a quiet pint and initially refused York's challenges, but word was getting round the docks and people were appearing to see what the fuss was about. At 5:00 both men and a substantial crowd left the pub and went around to the Guild Pitts. This was an area of rough ground behind Bridge Street, roughly where Guild Street now is. Isaac Barnett helped the two men take off their shirts and George Morris acted as the referee. There wasn't a proper ring or clock. They slugged it out in round after round, no gloves, no bells, and Jackson was getting the worst of it. He was probably

There were huge prizes for a skilled prizefighter. Strand Magazine

relieved when John Handy, the town constable turned up to see what the huge crowd was doing.

John Handy only had a limited jurisdiction. He could and did stop the fight whilst it was taking place within the borough

Prizefighting was a spectator sport with large wagers. It also offered a quick way out of poverty if you won. Strand Magazine

boundary. However, there was nothing he could do when the whole crowd, pugilists and all, walked across the bridge and re-started the fight in the field on the other side of the river. York redoubled his efforts to beat Jackson resorting not only to massive blows to the head, but even biting him when he thought Morris wasn't looking.

If you lost, there was precious little available in the way of medical care. Strand Magazine

William Jackson was now getting the worst of the fight. By 6:00 he had been knocked down several times and he only managed a couple more rounds before William York knocked him out. George Morris and several other spectators helped him to his feet and they took him to the stables at the back of the *Golden Lion* in Bridge Street to wash him down. There John Gardner, the landlord, settled him down with a glass of brandy and water in the kitchen. Despite the wash in the stables, Jackson was still bleeding from a severe cut just above his eye. John went about his business in the coaching inn but when he went back to the kitchen around 9:00 he found Jackson fast asleep at the kitchen table. He woke him up and took him upstairs to bed. Jackson was getting more comfortable and managed to undress himself, apart from getting his socks off, which John Gardener had to help him with. John left him at about 10:00, apparently in good health.

Life in the coaching inn started early; John Gardner went up to see how William Jackson was at twenty to five the next morning. He was stone dead. The surgeon David Price was called and performed an autopsy. Although superficially only suffering a bad cut above his eye, inside his brain was massively damaged, bone fragments had flaked off behind the injury, shredding the blood vessels. His career as a boxer had left his brain dreadfully scarred and this last pounding had opened an old wound.

William York, George Morris and Isaac Barnett were all arrested for manslaughter and after being held in the town

Today, the pub at the bottom of Bridge Street is called The Encore, *but it was known as* The Anchor *until the 1960s. It was a pretty rough place, frequented by the dockers and boatmen working on the canal and river.* The author

lock-up for a couple of days, were transferred to Warwick Gaol to await their trial. Luckily for them, David Price's autopsy was sufficient evidence to prove their innocence, William's death was an accident, simply the inevitable result of the previous bare knuckle fights.

Such fights were pretty common, and often ended up with a corpse. In the small village of Wolverton, not far from Snitterfield, a couple of years earlier, an afternoon's horseplay got out of hand. William Bartlam and George Dyke were larking about throwing water at each other on a warm April day. George got a bit over excited and challenged William to a proper bare-knuckle fight. At first William was having none of it, but George's wife waded in and started calling him a coward. William returned to the street outside the *Red House* and the fight began. Thomas Bartlam, William's brother, acted as his second, and Thomas Malin was the second for George. The fight went on for a fair while, watched by Mr Findon of the *Red House*. Eventually everyone was tired and wanted to stop, apart from George's wife who kept egging him on. It was a bad move as George eventually collapsed under a hail of punches from William. They dragged him back to his house and called the local surgeon. Mr Watson may not have been quite up to his job ... he looked over George's wounds, bled him and said he would be fine. A very short while later George died. The post-mortem revealed massive injuries to his brain and internal bleeding.

Naturally, William, his brother and Thomas Malin were charged with manslaughter. At the next Assizes William was found guilty, and the other two acquitted. The offence didn't seem to strike anyone as very serious, and William was fined one shilling. Life was cheap and medical techniques were somewhat primitive.

Surgeon David Price's evidence was not always taken as gospel. On 1 August 1834 Priscilla Gibbins died after she slipped and fell on the knife that she had picked up during the course of a quarrel with her husband, William Gibbins, the boat builder. The Gibbins family appear to have had the two dry docks that now lie beneath the theatre and lived in one of the Waterside cottages. That evening William and Priscilla had an almighty row, witnessed only by their son. The inquest heard how Priscilla grabbed a kitchen knife and rushed across the room to have a go at her husband, but tripped and fell, the knife sinking deep into her, causing death almost instantly. David Price was asked to examine the wound to see if William and his son were telling the truth. His comment was that the account of the stabbing was very improbable, if not actually impossible judging by the nature and angle of the wound. His evidence was simply ignored and William's story accepted by the magistrates. How Priscilla really died remains a mystery.

The boatmen faced far worse dangers than the towns' constable or demented wives. In particular the children were at risk. George Barnett, nephew of the boatman Isaac Barnett, (involved in the fatal fracas at *The Anchor*) accidentally drowned in the canal in July 1839. At nine years old he would have been expected to work alongside adults. Samuel Finday never made it that far; he fell off his father's boat, the *Mary Ann*, in the canal basin in July 1847. He was only five.

Even though this era was the start of the industrial revolution, South Warwickshire remained almost entirely an agricultural district. Life for farm workers was extremely difficult most of the time, and virtually impossible when the economy took one of its periodic nosedives.

Some things just never seem to change. England has always used migrant labour and it works fine when everything is booming, but when times get hard it is a recipe for trouble. The nineteenth century saw agricultural booms and busts on a regular basis. The Napoleonic Wars were a good time for farmers, although not so good for the labourers, but once the wars ended the whole economy slumped and farmers looked for cheaper labour. Thousands of Irishmen flooded onto the labour market, driven by extreme poverty in Ireland. The ordinary workers in England saw their jobs vanishing and their wages cut, across the country riots broke out, hay ricks set ablaze. It was 1830 and the time of the Captain Swinger riots and South Warwickshire was not exempt.

All through the summer there were cases of arson and by 6 August matters had reached boiling point in the village of Illmington. Thomas Edden decided he would employ a dozen cheap Irish labourers to get the harvest in. They were to sleep in the barns and work on his fields at the foot of the hill. As they set off to work that morning a crowd gathered, following them through the village muttering darkly about them taking their jobs. First one stone, and then a hail of rocks were thrown at them. The Irishmen dropped their tools and fled back to the farm for sanctuary. A mob of about fifty furious men was chasing them. Through the hot afternoon an uneasy stand off developed. George Dumbleton roused his workmates James Hathaway, William Cattle, William Foster and James Butler. They armed themselves with bludgeons, sticks and pitchforks. At about six o'clock they were joined by George Handy, David Jones and at least ninety other people.

Thomas Edden looked out of his farmhouse to see the Irish men cowering in terror in the barn. Surrounding the farm a huge mob started throwing rocks and baying for blood. His own family were just as terrified and they sent for the village constable. Unbelievably, the constable managed to diffuse the tense stand off. Wisely he waited a few days before getting reinforcements and then arresting all seven of the ringleaders.

This may have been the first trouble that south Warwickshire had with Irish labourers, but it certainly wasn't the last. Some years later another gang of labourers was employed at Gipsy Hall Farm in Wilmcote. It was the summer of 1853 and the gang had a reputation of hard drinking after their day's work in the bean fields. In the quiet little village their presence was not welcome, especially when they piled out of the pub at midnight shouting and singing. Thomas Bonehill made the fatal mistake of going out to tell them to shut up. Their racket had already roused the constable and he was running up the road to restore the peace. Of the six Irishmen one had had far too much to drink. Thomas Coulon confronted by Thomas Bonehill, lost his temper and lashed out with the bean hoe he was carrying. In an instant he smashed the hoe onto Thomas's head three times. Thomas didn't have time to react, the first blow fractured his skull, the second smashed the iron bow from the hoe and the third broke its blade, leaving a jagged shard embedded two inches into his skull.

The constable arrived as Thomas Bonehill collapsed to the ground. A few other people had been roused by the commotion and dragged him indoors as the constable arrested Coulon. The doctor arrived the next day and extracted the shard of metal from Thomas's head. He was dreadfully injured but still alive. He lingered part paralysed and in agony for months. Thomas Coulon was sentenced to eighteen months hard labour for the attack. He was lucky not to be executed because the following June Thomas Bonehill finally died from a secondary infection. Coulon was charged with manslaughter. The surgeon could not be certain that the death was a direct result of the attack and it was on this basis that Coulon managed to escape the ultimate penalty for his vicious and unprovoked attack.

CHAPTER 7

The Wandering Jew
1843
... it was the frantic shrieks of a dying man.

Binton Bridges, a cold dark night in February 1843. There was no orange sodium glow in the sky blotting out the stars; they burnt with their hard changeless brilliance. The water swirled unseen through the narrow arches. Then there was no traffic noise; you could hear a vixen calling a dog fox for miles. A chimney sweep cowered in terror in the hovel on Mr Day's land, what he had heard was no vixen, it was the frantic shrieks of a dying man. Mr William Vincent heard them in Welford and Henry Osborn in Binton. Closer to the bridges, Joseph Spencer shuddered in the cabin of his boat at the dreadful cries of murder. Strangely enough, Phoebe Walton, landlady of the *New Inn* by the bridge, heard nothing at all.

The following morning Joseph Spencer finished his voyage at Bidford and reported to his master and the owner of the boat, Mr Hindley. By now the nocturnal screams had been widely discussed. There seemed to be no doubt that a horrible murder had been committed at Binton Bridges. The gossip was that a Jew had been killed, although which Jew was unclear. There was one that kept a stall at Evesham market, but it didn't seem to be him. There was another, known only as Herman, who had an itinerant lifestyle and occasionally spent the night at local pubs like the *New Inn* at Binton Bridges. Herman had been in the *New Inn* that evening.

The boats on the river that year were a mixed lot. Mr Hindley's boat, steered by Joseph Spencer, was engaged on the coal run; travelling up the river to Stratford and then up the canal to the coalfields of the Black Country. William Ballard, the butcher and corndealer at North Littleton, owned another boat, the *Sweet Horne*. This boat was steered by Charles Harvey Bedenham. Charles had to employ Samuel Taylor, and occasionally Thomas Careless, Thomas Knight and a chap called Jones. The *Sweet Horne* was quite possibly a broad beam barge with a mast and sail, whilst Mr Hindley's boat was almost certainly a narrow boat, capable of navigating the canals. Joseph Spencer tied his boat up at the old wharf near Binton Bridges and in the afternoon before the unexplained screams, saw the *Sweet Horne* passing by. Joseph clearly heard the voice of Bedenham on the boat, and noticed that there were four people on board. He seems to have kept his head down whilst the *Sweet Horne* passed. There was a good reason for this; the crews of the riverboats had a fearsome reputation for violence.

The narrow boats of 1843 were the long distance juggernauts of their day. Their crews were respected. The canal system, virtually brand new, had yet to experience competition from the railways, and the owners and crews were well paid. Magnificent carthorses hauled boats around England, groomed and dressed to perfection. The River Avon navigation was far removed from this new efficient transport system; it was already over two centuries old, battered by floods and ruined by a lack of maintenance. The locks were dilapidated and some of them were utterly lethal to use. There was no towpath for the horses and gangs of men dragged the boats by hand when the wind failed. These men tended to be the very dregs of society, willing to do this arduous and dangerous work in return for enough cash to get drunk.

The spring and summer of 1843 passed with no further developments regarding the apparent murder. The harvest came and went with no news apart from the singular absence of Herman, the Jew. Thomas Knight took up lodgings with the Davis family in North Littleton. He had a guilty secret gnawing at his soul.

Hannah Davis and Thomas Knight were chatting away in the house in March 1844 when Thomas mentioned he had only a shilling left in his pocket:

Once upon a time I had twenty pounds in my pocket.
    Thomas, then it was not your own then?
    No it was not, nor should I wish to come by it as I came by that. I am better contented by this one shilling than when I had the twenty pounds.

How did you come by it?

We were drinking at Binton Bridges and there was a little Jew fellow in the house and Samuel Taylor was threatening all the while he was in the house how he would serve him. There was Harvey Bedenham, Thomas Careless, Samuel Taylor and myself. After a bit the little Jew went out and Taylor followed him and knocked him down on the bridge and just as he revived we all went up and the Jew said if they would not hurt him he would give them five pounds. Bedenham spoke up and said Damn my heart if we will not have the whole ruck. Then Sam Taylor fell to kicking him.

What did you do with him? asked Hannah. *Did you take him into the boat?*

Yes, for a time, and we had twenty pounds in money, and there was a roll of bills but they were numbered and we would not have them. We took what we had a mind out of the box and left the rest in.

What did you do with the man?

We did that to him and sunk him in the water where he would never be found. I took that twenty pounds to Stratford and Harvey Bedenham took it off me. I had none of it other than what I had to eat and drink. We stopped four days in Stratford.

Hannah told her husband, William, what Knight had said.

Knight, I should think that is not the truth, I cannot believe it, he told him.

You might believe it, for it is the truth. And Knight repeated the story to William, adding that Careless had cried out *For God's sake don't hurt the man* just before Sam Taylor kicked him to death.

William asked what they did with the body and Knight said that they threw him into a deep place in the river just below the bridges opposite a gut place.

Thomas, that man would have come up in seven or eight days when his gall burst.

No said Thomas, *he will never come up for we put that on him that he will never come up.*

What did you put on him?

We fetched a large stone off the wall which we tied with a pitch rope which we had off the boat and tied it onto the Jew and threw him into the deep hole just below the bridge.

What did you do with the Jew's box?

I had twenty pounds, but there was a lot of bills but we durst not have them because they were numbered. We put the bills in the box, tied the box to the body and threw it into the river. I took the twenty pounds to Stratford and we were four days spending it.

What did the Jew say when you were murdering him?

He made many grim faces, and then he spread his hands. I think the Lord will forgive me for I never put a hand towards murdering him.

William Davis didn't really believe the story at first, but over the succeeding weeks Knight repeated it several times and William asked his friend Thomas Waters, the village baker, what he thought of the tale. The cat was now out of the bag. Thomas Waters, being a baker, did his business with William

A private house today, this building used to be a small pub serving the boatmen travelling along the river as well as travellers on the road to Evesham. The author

Ballard the corn dealer and owner of the *Sweet Horne*. It was not long before the rumours of Knight's tale reached the ears of Charles Bedenham.

Bedenham turned up at the Davis's house on a July night at eleven o'clock. He hammered on the door until Hannah woke up and peered out of the window. William went down to the front door and asked what all the fuss was about. Bedenham demanded to see Knight. William told him that Knight had gone away for a while:

> *I will find him if I can and will break every bone in his skin if I can get hold of him for, Damn 'em, they used to steal fowls and bring them to the boat and I threatened to drown them for it. I believe there is something worse going forward but it was not I that did it.*

Bedenham called again, and threatened to beat Knight up when he found him. Knight had taken himself off to seek advice from a school teacher since matters were getting out of his control. Thomas Waters had not only spoken to William Ballard, but also to the policeman at Bretforton. George Smith decided this was no idle tale and went to the Davis's cottage to find out the truth. When he first arrived he spoke to William about the stories circulating about the murder. William was very reluctant to get involved, or make things worse for his lodger and so refused to tell him anything. George Smith was not to be dissuaded, and returned to the cottage when William was out. At his first visit Hannah was just as reluctant as her husband, but on his second visit she told him the whole story as she had heard it from Knight.

George Smith obtained a warrant for the arrest of Knight, Bedenham, Careless and Taylor. The first three he apprehended without difficulty, but Samuel Taylor had left the *Sweet Horne* the previous Easter and was only caught the day before the magistrate's inquiry.

The Stratford constable and some farm hands dragged the river below Binton Bridges. The river here is wide and deep, with even deeper holes carved by the turbulence from the bridges. They failed to find any trace of the missing Herman.

Welford and Binton, from the O S map of 1888. Courtesy of Ordnance Survey

Phoebe Walton of the *New Inn* flatly refused to give any kind of evidence that might implicate her or the pub,

> *I never, as I recollect, seeing him [Bedenham] in companionship with the two others at our house at a late hour of the night. I don't*

know a man called Samuel Taylor, nor Thomas Careless ... I have never seen a Jew or a traveller in the house when Bedenham has been drinking there.

The magistrates were in a dilemma. Knight's story was consistent with the vanishing of the Jew, but not only was there no body or other corroborative evidence, Knight himself was described as 'flighty' by William Ballard and Phoebe Walton seemed very certain that the gang had never been in the *New Inn*. With only hours to go before the start of the Warwick Assizes, the magistrates decided that there was insufficient evidence and let the matter drop.

Binton Bridges have a chequered history. There used to be a timber toll-bridge but it was so rickety that it had to be replaced with a proper stone bridge in the eighteenth century. Somewhere under the water lie the remains of an itinerant Jew. The author

CHAPTER 8

The Jackdaw
1872
Hannah! Hannah! I am stabbed, I am dying!

The jackdaw has a somewhat mischievous reputation and a penchant for stealing bright things. In the autumn of 1871 the butcher, Edward Handcock, was baffled by the disappearance of his sticking knife. He was completely alone, working as he did as a jobbing butcher, cutting up a pig he had just killed. He put the knife down, turned around and then it was gone, spirited away in an instant. He returned to his dilapidated hovel in the village of Priors Hardwick a very angry man.

Edward Handcock was almost always angry. He started life reasonably well off, owning a house and butcher's business in the village, married to one of the village girls. This happy state did not last, as he was jealous of his wife, suspecting her of being unfaithful and beating her up when he was in drink. He drank quite a lot, gradually descending into poverty. His first wife died and he remarried, but still he was insanely jealous, still he drank himself into the ground. His second wife also died and by now rumours were circulating round the village that he had beaten her to death in one of his frequent rages, but nothing was proved. He remarried once more, this time to the sister of his first wife who had an illegitimate son. He was forty-three and she thirty-two at the time of their wedding in 1865. He had four children by his first marriages. By now his property was all gone and the family lived in a tiny hovel, one of a row of flimsy dwellings that served as scant protection from the elements. The one room downstairs was for cooking and washing, two rooms upstairs for the whole family.

Strangely enough, the young son of his new wife was accidentally killed by a plough falling on him. 1871 was not proving to be a good year for his wife Betsy. She had been

Edward Handcock gradually descended into a pit of drunken anger and jealousy, losing his house, his business and his sanity. Strand Magazine

married to Edward for six years and his rages and jealousies were getting worse; the death of her son seemed to be an accident, but who could tell what really happened? 1872 saw no improvement in his attitude and fearing for her safety Betsy started to hide all the knives in the house.

Edward was called back to the village where he had mysteriously lost his sticking knife to slaughter another pig. It was 13 November 1872 and Edward had a few extra drinks to fortify himself before killing the pig. He had to use the knives in the farm because Betsy had hidden all of his own. Ominously it was now that the jackdaw chose to return his sticking knife. He tucked it away in his pocket.

Edward went back to his hovel in Priors Hardwick. He had even more to drink once he had been paid for his work. He was still maniacally jealous of his wife; only the day before he had told Reverend Hallett of his suspicions. The vicar had tried to persuade him that his fears were groundless; Betsy was not having an affair with anyone. Edward was not convinced, in his mind he was sure she was in and out of bed with almost everyone in the village. Half drunk he banged in through the door and promptly started an argument with Betsy. She was used to him ranting at her once he had a few beers inside him, but this time he seemed positively malicious. She said she was going to get the police from the next village and went out. Inside the squalid room Edward took out the knife and started sharpening it. He ignored his eldest son Walter and went upstairs to wait for her.

Out in the street Betsy met one of her neighbours and persuaded her to go and fetch the constable. The neighbour promised to do so and Betsy returned home to get the children ready for bed. Unfortunately the neighbour changed her mind about the errand because the couple quarrelled so often, perhaps it was just another one of their blazing rows which would blow over in a few hours, no need to call the police again.

Back in the house Betsy undressed the three little children and remarked to Walter that she expected a pretty row when she went upstairs. She went up to the front room with the little ones and together with Eliza, her six-year-old daughter, settled them into bed. Edward burst out of the other room and before Betsy even had time to cry out, stabbed her several times, slipping the knife into her leg and twisting it viciously. Betsy screamed out in agony and hammered on the thin partition wall for help from next door:

Hannah! Hannah! I am stabbed, I am dying!

In his blind rage Edward threw her onto the bed and she shouted to her son:

Walter, Walter, he is cutting me.

She reeled up from the bed only to fall down the stairs, bleeding profusely. Hannah Hart and John Haynes rushed in from next door to find her lying head downwards on the stairs. *He has stabbed me,* Betsy whispered.

They tried to staunch the bleeding and get a drop of spirits down her. John raced off to raise the alarm and get a surgeon.

Betsy Handcock was tended by her neighbours as she slowly bled to death. Strand Magazine

The local constable was summoned and found Edward Handcock cowering in the bedroom:

Edward, Edward, what have you done, your wife is dying?
I have done it was his only reply.
Sergeant Webb arrived soon after.
I suppose you are going to take me, Edward muttered.

Betsy slipped into unconsciousness and by the time the surgeon arrived she had bled to death; the knife wound had severed the femoral artery.

Sergeant Webb did indeed take Edward Handcock, all the way to the gallows via Warwick Assizes. In the weeks before his execution he repented and sought solace in the Wesleyan Ministry. He sought no reprieve from his sentence of hanging, and on Tuesday 7 January 1873, faced Mr J Smith of Manchester, the state executioner. He had brandy and water for breakfast. The execution was to take place inside Warwick Gaol since a law of 1863 had banned public executions. A few county and prison officials and eight members of the press were present. At 8:00 am the trap fell from under his feet, the noose tightened and he was gradually strangled. It took four minutes to kill him. Outside a black flag was hoisted to signify that justice was done. An hour later the body of Edward Handcock was cut down and buried inside the prison grounds.

CHAPTER 9

The Drybank Farm Murder
1897
He remembered the box being quite heavy.

George Brandish of Drybank Farm, Ettington, had a sister by the name of Elizabeth. She was a nurse who had secured a job in Kent. In 1895 she had a brief liaison with an unknown man and had a child as a result. The little boy was to prove a serious liability to her career as a nurse. He was christened Rees Thomas Yells Brandish and when only nine months old, Elizabeth arranged for him to be brought up by the Post family who lived in the village of Wye near Ashford, telling virtually no one about his existence. Elizabeth paid five shillings a week to cover the expenses. In an effort to keep the existence of this bastard child secret, she told them that her surname was Edwards. It was the young niece of the Posts, Sarah Urben, that actually cared for the toddler, bringing him up as though he was her own child. The months passed by with regular letters from Elizabeth inquiring as to the health of the lad and prompt payments for his maintenance. One typical letter went:

> *I have not forgotten my darling little boy. I would give my life to see him. I am always thinking of him. I know God will look over him and care for him. He is all I have to care for. My parents and all I love are gone but him… I do not know what I should do if anything happened to him.*

Although Elizabeth wrote regularly to either Mr & Mrs Post or to Sarah herself, she never managed to make a personal visit to see the little boy. Rees thrived in the care of Sarah, putting on weight and growing up normally.

Elizabeth secured herself a new position as nurse in the Midlands and in August 1896 moved to Holy Cross, Clent, where she lodged with Mrs Shivlock, a widow. It was here that she met Sergeant Narramore, the local policeman. They had met when Elizabeth nursed his wife during her last illness. After she died they gradually formed a close acquaintance and were often seen walking out together in the village. The problem for Elizabeth was simple enough; he would not marry her if he found out that she had a bastard child. By the summer of 1897 their relationship had grown to the point where he was seriously contemplating marriage. Once a year had passed since the death of his wife, he would be able to propose to her without incurring the disapproval of the village. This possible proposal was both a blessing and a curse for Nurse Elizabeth Brandish.

Although the letters and money arrived regularly at the Post household, they were all surprised when Elizabeth Edwards turned up on 8 September 1897 with the intention of collecting the child and taking the boy back to Drybank Farm to see Elizabeth's family and friends. Sarah Urben noticed that inside Elizabeth's cloak was a name label marked 'E. Brandish'. During that evening Sarah's aunt and Elizabeth discussed what clothes she should take, whether they could be fitted into the pram and wrapped up in the sheet of white macintosh material that Elizabeth had brought with her. No, Elizabeth was quite adamant that the white cloth could not be used as it belonged to her people. Elizabeth stayed the night with the Posts and the next morning went into Ashford and bought a round tin travelling box for 2s 9d, leaving it at the shop, Messrs Lee & Sons, saying that she would collect it the next day. That afternoon, Elizabeth returned to the Posts' house and packed a few items of Rees's clothes. Little Rees was suffering from whooping cough and there was a long discussion as to whether the children at Drybank Farm had had the disease, Elizabeth thought not, and whether it was a sensible idea to take him there. Elizabeth seemed more concerned that the child would be awkward during the long journey.

On the morning of 10 September Sarah Urben accompanied Elizabeth and Rees to Ashford. Rees stayed with Sarah while Elizabeth went and collected the tin trunk. She

Drybank Farm on the ancient Fosse Way, not far from Ettington, was the place where Elizabeth Brandish buried her son. Local legend has it that the cabbages always grow well there, which, since she buried him in quicklime, may be accurate.
The author

showed it to Sarah who noticed that it was empty and lightweight. Sarah then saw them board the train bound for London. She was sad to see the little boy go off into the unknown with a mother who had never once visited him. She insisted that Elizabeth write to her with news of the child. Elizabeth said that she would, and that if she decided to keep the child at Drybank, she would send for the rest of his clothes. Sarah watched Rees, dressed with a blue sailor's hat, and fawn jacket with smoked pearl buttons, clamber into the carriage. In a cloud of steam and smoke the train bore the little boy out of her life forever.

Sergeant Cockshaw, of the Metropolitan Police, was alerted by a Mrs Ada Turner to a woman in difficulty at five that afternoon. She found Elizabeth slumped on the tin trunk with little Rees beside her just outside a coffee house in Melton Street. She was in a right state, smelling of brandy and vomit. Elizabeth seemed incoherent and had been trying to find a room in a hotel, but picked a house of ill repute. Ada Turner thought that she might have been drugged and so felt it important to take her and the child to a Police Station. There Elizabeth stated that she had drunk some brandy at Euston Station which was too strong for her, and that the little boy was travel sick. Sergeant Cockshaw called the police surgeon, Dr Maughan and the police matron, Mrs Pickles. They tidied her up as best they could and tried to find out where she was from. Elizabeth gave her name as Edwards again, but would not give her address or any relatives. Mrs Pickles washed the child and made sure that they both had something to eat. Mrs Pickles then escorted Elizabeth to Euston Station and made sure that she got on the right train, this time bound for Bletchley. Sergeant Cockshaw watched Elizabeth and Rees together with the parcel of clothes and tin trunk safely depart.

They arrived at Bletchley that afternoon and went to the *Railway Hotel*. Alice Snape, the chambermaid, found the child very distressed and crying. She gave him some lemonade in the coffee room and then the nurse and child spent the night in one of the rooms. Alice woke them up on the morning of the 11th and by 8 o'clock they were ready to go out. Rees seemed much better after his rest.

Elizabeth Brandish and the little boy were next seen by James Owen, the Station Master, at Towcester. It was 4:45 that afternoon. It was memorable because the train had actually arrived on time. This was very unusual for the East & West Junction Railway. The railway, now mostly destroyed, was one of the many rural lines run on a shoestring and limping from crisis to crisis. Its timetable was a standing joke across the Midlands. It ran via a few small stations from Towcester to Broom. Nurse Brandish asked James Owen if she could upgrade her 3rd class ticket to a 2nd class, and pay the excess. Her reason was that the little boy was fretful and would annoy the other passengers. James Owen placed her in one of the 2nd class compartments and told John Days, the guard, that she was there. The carriage was not a corridor type so that once the train set off, Elizabeth and Rees were alone and could not be interrupted.

The train lurched off towards Stratford at 7:19. John Days checked the train at Blakesley, and saw Rees kneeling on the seat facing him, Nurse Brandish sitting beside him. There was

East & West Junction trains were notoriously slow. Shakespeare Birthplace Trust Record Office

no one else in the compartment. Losing time all along, the ancient engine was barely capable of running itself let alone a passenger train, the guard allowed just sixty seconds at each stop. At Kineton the curtains on the carriage were drawn. At 8:24 the train pulled into Ettington Station and by the time John Days got to the carriage, the door was already open, the tin trunk on the platform and Nurse Brandish was dragging a white bundle out of the compartment. She headed for the Waiting Shed with it under her arm. Of the child he saw no sign. With only sixty seconds and the train already late, he blew his whistle and set off for Stratford.

William Hooton, the signalman and porter noticed Elizabeth Brandish, and thought that the bundle she had under her arm was a suckling child. She left the station for Drybank Farm with the bundle. Before leaving she asked John Henry Heritage, the local carrier, to take the trunk on his cart up to Drybank Farm. He found that the trunk was heavy when he lifted it onto the wagon.

Elizabeth Brandish stayed briefly with her brother at Drybank Farm. On Monday 13 September she set off for Clent. James Southam, the village blacksmith picked up the tin trunk and took it and the nurse back to the station. Elizabeth and her luggage made their way to Hagley Station where Evan George Edwards collected her. He put the tin trunk in the back of his brake and they set off for Holy Cross. Elizabeth got off at the police station to see Sergeant Narramore and Evan took the trunk on to Mrs Shivlock's house. As Mrs Shivlock was out, he left the trunk with Mrs Weston next door. Later that afternoon the two old ladies dragged the trunk into Mrs Shivlock's kitchen. Elizabeth Brandish seems to have spent the night with Sergeant Narramore and only returned to her lodgings on the Tuesday. On the Wednesday morning Elizabeth and Mrs Shivlock carried the heavy trunk up to Elizabeth's bedroom. Later that day Elizabeth wrote a note to Sarah Urben saying the baby was well and staying at Drybank Farm.

On Thursday morning Elizabeth decided she had forgotten something and had to return to Drybank Farm. Mrs Shivlock once again helped her drag the tin trunk downstairs and they heaved it onto a wall so that the carrier Frederick Norris could get it into his cart en route for the station. He remembered the box being quite heavy. Elizabeth returned to Clent the following day. Frederick remembered that the box was now clearly empty. Of the little boy Rees there was still no sign.

Sarah Urben was puzzled by the first letter and then alarmed by a second one from Elizabeth. The description of the baby seemed all at odds with the child she had raised. She wrote to the local vicar asking if he could visit Drybank to see if they were looking after the child. Elizabeth's sister-in-law, Mrs Brandish, was surprised at the visit; she knew nothing of Rees. Sarah Urben was deeply alarmed at the absence of the child. She alerted the police.

It took some time for the police to follow up Sarah's concerns. On 17 October Sergeant Pugh went to interview Elizabeth Brandish at Clent. She told him how she had met a woman on the Clent Hills in the summer and fallen into conversation with her. The woman was childless and would dearly love to have a baby. Elizabeth decided that this would be the solution to her problems paying for the maintenance of Rees, and the two of them travelled down to Ashford. The unknown woman stayed in the town whilst Elizabeth collected the child. They travelled back together on the route already described, except that the un-named woman was in a different carriage on the East & West Junction train. After Ettington they went their separate ways; the woman took Rees with her. Elizabeth did not know the woman's name or address. This woman did not pay her anything for the child and she had no idea where this unknown foster mother and the child were now. Sergeant Pugh went off to see if he could track down the child and this unknown character, but first he went and had a long talk with Sergeant Narramore.

Sergeant Narramore then had a long talk with Elizabeth on 22 October. She convinced him that she had acted properly and had made the best choice for the baby. He thought that her act of giving the child away was practical, if somewhat foolish. Two days later Mrs Weston noticed something odd. Mrs Shivlock was out and Elizabeth closed the curtains of the house during the afternoon, after peering furtively out. Then a thick column of smoke appeared from the chimney. Another unusual event was that she asked Sergeant Narramore to paint the inside of her tin trunk because it was getting rusty after she had done some washing in it.

The search for the strange woman and little Rees brought no joy. Elizabeth continued her work as a nurse with Mrs Shivlock. Sarah Urben became even more worried about the fate of the child she had raised. Sergeant Pugh was finding his investigation constantly pointing to one conclusion and he called in the help of Detective Inspector Ravenhall. A week later Elizabeth Brandish was arrested for the suspected murder of Rees Thomas Yells Brandish.

On her arrest Elizabeth had a letter in her pocket addressed to Sergeant Narramore:

I feel very low-spirited. My head seems to give way and I feel as if I was going mad. I am so sorry, dear, to have brought this sorrow on you and the girls after what we have all been to one another for nearly eleven months. You and I have lived for one another and the girls and we have been as one. I have never found as true a friend before as you and until my end, come however it may; I love you with my whole being. What ever wrong has been in my life has not been of my own seeking. It is misfortune. God knows I have tried hard and fast to do right, and night and day pray that whatever happens His hand may guide and help me. I feel, although innocent, I cannot clear myself. My one great trouble is my dearest brother and his family may be brought into trouble through me. I swear they know nothing of my affairs, and I hope, dear, if anything unforeseen ever happens, and I am called away, you will take charge of everything belonging to me, and take it to your house, and if I should die, remember to put me in your grave and see to my burial.

The letter convinced Detective Ravenhall to have a close look at Drybank Farm. Elizabeth was now incarcerated in Warwick Gaol and was sending letters to Sergeant Narramore's daughter asking for fresh clothes and a bag of money she had left with her. The letter of 15 November had a postscript:

Since writing the above something has transpired, please ask your father to come and see me immediately.

Something had indeed transpired, on 13 November Detective Inspector Ravenhall had been digging up the garden of Drybank Farm and discovered the body of a child buried in a pit with quicklime. The corpse was taken to the *Chequers Inn* where Sarah Urben was waiting for news. The poor girl could not positively identify the body, it was so badly decomposed, but the hair seemed to be the right colour and the number of teeth the same. Dr William Walter Fenton proceeded with an autopsy to try and ascertain the cause of death, but found it almost impossible. The child may have been suffocated, but he couldn't be positive. It was a truly gruesome task.

A telegram arrived at the village from Warwick Gaol. On being told of the discovery Elizabeth wired a brief statement:

My brother or wife know nothing. Will make statement.

The coroner's inquest decided that Elizabeth Brandish should stand trial for the wilful murder of the child, but at the subsequent trial it could not be proved that the body found at Drybank was really that of Rees, nor that a murder had been committed – the baby may well have simply died – it was all too common in those days. The jury was split evenly. A second trial took place in July 1898, amid a blaze of publicity and speculation, and this jury found Elizabeth not guilty of wilful murder. The lesser charges of manslaughter or neglect could not now be brought and she walked free. Sergeant Narramore never replied to any of her letters.

CHAPTER 10

The Compton Verney Tragedy
1903
... and the Lord have mercy on your soul.

Compton Verney is a large rural mansion. Today it is a prestigious art gallery set amid glorious gardens landscaped by Capability Brown. There is an ornamental lake with an elegant little bridge forming an impressive approach to the house itself. Mature exotic trees and bushes form a pleasant venue for art workshops, picnics and modern leisure. The place has been settled for a thousand years, but some strange quirk of fate seems to have prevented it from ever blooming into a town. The Normans expanded the Saxon village, and it became Compton Murdak, named after the family that owned the manor. Unlike most English villages the name was changed when the Verney family took over the estate in 1435. The Verneys managed to claim a barony and with the associated wealth expanded the manor house. The 12th Baron Willoughby de Broke improved and modernised the place. The 14th Baron did the same again, this time hiring Lancelot Brown to turn the grounds from formal gardens into the romantic vision of Arcadia that was all the rage in the mid-eighteenth century. The fortunes of the Barons of Willoughby de Broke faded during the nineteenth century as a deep economic depression slashed farm incomes. The magnificent house had to be rented out by the 19th Baron. The landscape gradually matured and in 1903 the grounds looked much as they do now, apart from the blood splattered across the grass.

Harriett Ann Devall was the head laundry maid of Compton Verney. The house and its staff was almost a village in its own right, gardeners, valets, cooks and butler, all came together to form a small community dedicated to the maintenance of the house and its owner. Annie was twenty-six in 1903. She was a big strong girl; she needed to be to deal with the vast cauldrons of boiling washing. She was full of life and simply adored dancing.

Annie came from a Leamington family and was raised in Victoria Street. She learnt her skills as a laundry maid locally and eventually managed to secure a good position at Draycott House, near Chippenham in Wiltshire. It was here in the summer of 1902 that she met a young lad by the name of Walter George Couzens. Walter lived with his parents in the village of Draycott. He was only seventeen, but they got on well and by 1903 he had given her a ring and they were engaged.

Walter was a serious hard working young man. His education had been somewhat sporadic because he was a sickly child and prone to epileptic fits. He was intelligent though, and had not had any fits since leaving school. He was

The magnificent mansion and gardens at Compton Verney have recently been restored after a century of neglect. Lancelot 'Capability' Brown laid out the grounds, but they became the scene of the horrific murder of Annie Devall. The author

rather susceptible to deep bouts of depression. Walter worked as a farmhand and had a reputation as a good strong and sober worker, although with a slightly rash temper.

Annie worked hard at Draycott House, saving up enough of her wages to buy herself a bicycle. This may not sound much today, but in 1903 it was the equivalent value and status of a car, particularly considering the very poor wages for domestic servants. However, on 25 July Annie handed in her notice at Draycott House and spent a week staying with Walter and his family until she returned to her family in Leamington on 1 August. She had to leave the precious bicycle with Walter.

Walter himself thought he would try to get a better job and started to apply for positions on the railway. He approached the vicar, the Reverend R E Neville and his employer, the farmer Mr F G Ody, for references and they agreed to post them on to him at his new address. He moved to his uncle's house at Little Gaddeston, Great Berkhampstead, Hertfordshire. He managed to get all his clothes into a small trunk and cycle there on Annie's bike. He had still not managed to get a job by October. One reason for his lack of success was that he had slumped into a black depression when Annie left.

Annie Devall managed to secure the position of head laundry maid at the Compton Verney estate with comparative speed. She was exceptionally strong and jovial and blended into the little community with ease. There was one annoying element in her new life; Walter was not sending her bike to her despite repeated requests. The two were corresponding on a regular basis, although it seems Walter started to wonder if Annie wasn't starting to look closer to home for a little affection and fun.

She wrote to him with yet another request for the bicycle:

My Darling – I am a little hurt and upset at you saying 'perhaps there was someone that I liked better, but I have not seen them yet' I am sure that I have not given you any cause to say that, and I never thought of you 'sloping' as you say with the bicycle, for I always knew you would rather give to me rather than take from me. This is an outlandish spot so I am feeling fair miserable today… With fondest love and heaps of kisses, I remain your ever loving and affectionate lover, Nance. XXX

A further forty-seven kisses filled the corner of the page.

Their relationship was clearly under strain from the separation and from Walter's failure to return Annie's bicycle.

Walter really didn't help matters by forgetting to put a stamp on his next letter. Annie wrote back:

I see nowadays that men are a deceitful lot, and if you could not send my bike without forgiveness I am quite sure you cannot think so much about me as you say you do. I do not know whether to send love or not, but I will remain your ever loving Nance.

She put the unstamped letter in with this.

The unstamped letter came back with this note on it:

Misfortunes will happen, but I wish this had not. It can't be helped. It is too late, but the old fashioned saying Better late than never is not so with us Pet. Miserable Wal at present. The accompanying note continued 'When I opened my purse I could see what a fool I was, for I had the stamps in my purse. But, dear, I hope you will look over it … I think as much of you as ever I did, and I will keep my promise. I will never have another if I don't have you. I thought I had a friend last week, but I don't know what to make of it at present. If you will not have me I will soon see if I can't do for a soldier. I still remain yours if you will be mine, – Wal

Annie probably wasn't very impressed with this letter. If nothing else she had met one of the stable boys at Compton Verney, Tom Whitworth, and was finding life more fun with him. She wrote back to Walter:

Dear Wal, Just a line in answer to your letter. No doubt you will be surprised to get this from me, but really I must tell you that I feel I really could not keep true to you, for there are so many dances and concerts going on, and, when any chap asks me to go, I go, of course and you know I always like dancing, so I really could not give it up for anything. Also, I like plenty of life, so I go first with one and then another, and I know you are very jealous, so I thought I had better write and tell you. So I think the best thing for us to do is to part friends, for I would not like you to find me out at the last. But no doubt you will find another that will be more deserving of your love than I am, for I will say I flirt first with one and then with another. So I don't think I shall have another to stick to and then I shall cause no jealousy with anyone. Of course I shall leave it to you the way you like to take it. I am very sorry to do this, but really I must tell you about my flirting, and really, if you came down here, I really could not get out to see you. So I think I must close, – I remain yours sincerely, Nance.

The letter arrived at Little Gaddeston on the morning of Friday 30 October, along with the references Walter had requested. Heartbroken, he went up to his bedroom and changed into some travelling clothes, shoved a few things into

Suspicions were first raised when a bloodstained bicycle was found leaning on the bridge. Walter Couzens had fled into the night. The author

his pockets and at 9:00 he set off for Warwick with the bicycle. Taking the train and then cycling the remainder of the way he arrived at Compton Verney in the afternoon.

The first person Walter met along the drive to the big house was none other than Tom Whitworth. He directed Walter to the laundry. Inside, Annie looked up in surprise when she heard her bicycle bell ring. She invited Walter in for a cup of tea and they had a long conversation about their relationship. They took a walk in the grounds of the house for over an hour. Kate Usher, one of the housemaids, interrupted them at one point, and later saw Walter pedalling off down the long drive. All agog to know what had transpired, she pumped Annie for the gossip. Annie had explained things to Walter and he had seemed to take it all calmly enough. She had discreetly omitted to mention anything about Tom the stable hand as she thought Walter might do something rash, either killing himself or Tom. In all events they parted on reasonable terms and agreed to meet again the next evening by the ornamental bridge.

On the Saturday morning Annie sat down and wrote a letter to her sister, Adelaide, in Leamington:

> *… I must tell you I wrote to give that chap up. He landed here yesterday. I was surprised to see him. A straw would have knocked me down when I saw him, and the best of it was that Tom Whitworth directed him to the laundry. But I shall not have any more to do with him. I told him I should not give up my pleasure for any man. Of course he does not like my dancing or anything, so he can go to the devil for me. I offered him the ring back, but he would not take it. But I expect Tom and I will be coming home soon, so I can tell you all about it then. Don't forget my dancing shoes because Tom is going to take me to a dance next Tuesday. I have had to tell Tom all about it; he has taken it all in very good part.*

A very despondent Walter rode away from Compton Verney on Friday night. He reached the *Rose & Crown* in Kineton and asked for lodgings until Monday; telling Mr Ivens, the landlord, that he was visiting his sister who was the head laundry maid at Compton Verney. Mr Ivens put the bicycle in the stable for the night. Walter slumped on the bed in this unfamiliar country pub; he didn't even bother to get undressed. Saturday morning, as Annie was writing the note to her sister, Walter set off on the bike to see if he could find work in the vicinity.

Walter cycled to a farm near Compton Verney and asked the head groom if there was any work. William Hunt found him to be a pleasant enough young lad, who seemed delighted to find that there was two or three days work at three shillings a day. He set him working with the horses straight away. Walter returned to the pub for his lunch and then returned to Pittern Hill farm for the afternoon. He told Mr Hunt that he needed to finish by seven o'clock because he was meeting his sister at Compton Verney. He promised to be back at seven the next morning.

Annie Devall spent the Saturday working in the laundry as usual. One of her tasks was to show the new under laundry maid around the house and laundry. It was Emma Rouse's first day at work. At 7:45 pm she heard a bicycle bell ringing by the laundry door. It was Walter. The two of them fell into deep conversation. Emma overheard them as they were parting. Annie said to Walter: 'When I say No, I mean No.' It seems Walter was unable to convince Annie to come back to him. The two of them walked off into the grounds. In the gathering gloom of that Halloween night those were the last words anyone heard Annie Devall utter.

Harold Cox was cycling home from his job as clerk at Lloyds Bank in Warwick at about 8:15 when he noticed an unattended bicycle leaning against the parapet of the bridge. Thinking this a bit odd he called in at Kineton Police Station and reported it. It was sometime before PC Simpson got the time to investigate the matter. At 11:45 he found the bike still there, there was a bloodstained envelope addressed to Walter's uncle lying beside it. There were bloodstains on the handlebars, the bell and on the lower bracket. PC Simpson was then joined by PC Savage, and the two of them started to search along the road and into the grounds of Compton Verney. When they reached the ornamental bridge over the lake they found a belt draped over the parapet and a razor case lying on the ground. Matters were looking deeply suspicious and so PC Simpson took the bike back to Kineton Police Station whilst PC Savage decided to walk around the area. He woke up the butler at the lodge to ask if anyone was missing and the man agreed to check in the morning.

It was ten to two in the morning when PC Savage met a young man walking along the road towards Compton Verney, near Tithe Farm. He stopped him and enquired what his business was at such a late hour. The young man told him he was walking from Leamington to Kineton in search of work and that he was originally from Wiltshire. When the constable asked him what sort of work he was looking for the young man said he worked with horses. PC Savage suggested he try Kineton as that was where the County Hunt was based. There they parted. In the darkness of an overcast night PC Savage carried on from Bowshot crossroads towards Wellesbourne and the young man towards Kineton. Little did PC Savage know at the time, the young man was none other than Walter Couzens.

Before first light PC James Smith went to Compton Verney. He knew something was very amiss and in the cold dawn he spotted two bundles of letters floating in the water. He fished them out and found one bundle was the references that Walter had received by post on the Friday, the other was letters from Walter's sister. PC Smith then went up to the house to find out if there was anyone missing. Mrs Alice Jackson, the head housekeeper, told him that she did not see Annie the previous evening. It was her duty to see that all the maids were inside, but Annie had the keys to the laundry and was supposed to lock that up before retiring. As head laundry maid she was allowed a degree more freedom. However Emma Rouse had spent a restless first night at Compton Verney. She was supposed to be sharing a bedroom with Annie Devall, but Annie had not come in. PC Smith searched the room and found bundles of letters from Walter amongst Annie's things, but no sign of the girl herself. A policeman was despatched to Leamington to see if her parents had any idea of her whereabouts.

Fearing the worst, PC Smith set some of his colleagues to dragging the lake near the bridge and others searching the footpaths and woods. Police were arriving from all over the district by now. PC Smith started a detailed search of the grounds close to the house. Starting from the gate where Emma Rouse had last seen Annie, he followed the footpath. Spots of blood appeared on the path not far from the conservatory. He then found traces of blood, deep footprints and kicked up turf in the top corner of the lawn. It seemed as though there had been a ferocious struggle here, and he followed a trail of blood stained grass for seventeen yards towards a ditch. In the ditch he found the body of Annie Devall. She was lying on her side, head towards Kineton, with her throat dreadfully slashed by numerous cuts. Her head had almost been severed by the violence of the attack and a large pool of blood was congealing on the grass. On the bank lay a gore-encrusted razor. PC Smith found a note in her pocket, which read:

> *I do not mean to see you again. The best thing for you to do is to go back to your aunt.*

Realising the awful nature of the murder he sent a car to catch up with the policeman en route to Leamington and to convey

Walter appears to have dragged Annie's body to a ditch by the lake after rippng her throat open with a cut-throat razor. The author

the dreadful news to Annie's family. He then carried the corpse to the Racquet Room in the house until the doctor arrived. The hunt for the murderer was on by midday, and not surprisingly it was Walter George Couzens that the police wanted to interview as a matter of urgency.

Walter, although seemingly lucid during his midnight encounter with PC Savage, was now cut adrift in a hostile world. Through the night he tramped towards Warwick. At nine o'clock he met Thomas Davis and asked him if he knew what time the train to London was. Thomas thought that there was one after 11:00. Walter asked where he could get a drink and Thomas told him that all the town pubs would be shut until 12:30, but if he went to one of the country villages he could probably get one earlier. The two of them then walked out to Leek Wootton and had a pint there. While they were supping their beers Walter pulled out his cigarette case and offered Thomas one. Thomas was surprised that all the cigarettes were completely wringing wet. Walter said he had dropped them in a bucket of water the night before. Walter bought more whisky and beer for them both. On the way back Walter wondered where he could buy a new hat. Thomas took him to a shop he knew in West Street and there he bought a hard hat for 1s 6d. He put his old cap in his pocket. Thomas did not notice anything strange about the lad at all, and last saw him walking up to the station.

He turned up at the station at 2.15. Ernest Robins told him the next train to London was at 2:30. Walter sat down on the bench by the fire, but Ernest told him that he couldn't wait in the ticket office. Walter was directed to the waiting room and he left. After the train left Ernest found Walter still sitting in the waiting room. Walter said he had missed the train because it left early. Ernest told him it hadn't and crossly told him that he was closing the station until the evening train arrived at 6:56. Walter wandered off and returned at 5:50 to catch the London train.

Superintendent Cussack, now in charge of the investigation, realised that Walter had fled, sent a message to every police force in the country to try and apprehend him. Walter turned up at the *Lamb Inn* in Wootton Bassett on the evening of

2 November, booked a room and went to bed. The local policeman, Sergeant Rich, was called and arrested him at 10:40. Walter gave his name as Robins and denied anything to do with the murder. Sergeant Rich arranged for him to be taken to Swindon police station, where Detective Inspector Drakeley collected him.

Inspector Drakeley had been roused from his slumbers at 2:00 a.m. on the third and taken the train to Swindon. He was probably in no mood to be messed about by the time he met Couzens. The young man put up no pretence and admitted his identity. The two of them boarded a train back towards Kineton. During the long journey Walter asked the inspector,

'Have you seen the body of the girl?'

Drakeley replied, 'No, and now let me warn you that you are not obliged to say anything about the matter, but whatever you do say may be used in evidence'.

Walter continued:

I was only going to say this; When I met the girl on Saturday night I had no thought of hurting her in any way. I should not have done so only she begged me to do it. We walked down towards the lane and sat down on the grass under a tree. I was smoking a cigarette and she also smoked one. She said she wished she were dead and asked me to kill her. I told her not to talk such rubbish, and she placed her head on my shoulder and said, 'Cut my throat and finish me.' She begged so hard that I cut it, and afterwards I rolled her into the ditch.

The train rattled on towards Kineton. Walter asked if there was any news of his father. The Inspector told him he was very cut up about it; he had given Walter the razor that he had used to kill the girl. When the train finally arrived at Kineton Station an astonishing scene awaited them, the entire station and approach roads were thronged with people wanting to see the murderer. The police had trouble getting Walter through the crowds and into the comparative calm of the police station. There Walter was formally charged with the murder of Harriett Ann Devall. He replied to the charge:

She pressed me to do it. She placed her head on my shoulder and begged me to kill her.

Over the next week the coroner's inquest heard evidence from all the witnesses, including Walter's distraught father. The confession on the train left them with a choice between wilful murder and manslaughter. It took the jury five minutes to decide that this was a case of wilful murder and Walter was committed for trial at Warwick Assizes. In the meantime he was imprisoned in Warwick Gaol.

The trial commenced on Tuesday 8 December. Walter was brought into the dock, a pale and haggard figure. He sat holding a handkerchief to his face amid a packed courtroom. He appeared a pathetic and lonely lad, and aroused as much sympathy in the courtroom as loathing. His plea of Not Guilty was barely audible. Mr Parfitt for the prosecution detailed the grisly details of the killing and the events leading up to it. The defence lawyer, Mr S Dorset, attempted to prove that Walter was still suffering from a form of epilepsy, and was thus momentarily unaware of what he was doing. The arguments went on through the day and after eight hours the jury retired to consider their verdict. After nearly half an hour they returned and the foreman stood up and addressed Justice Channell:

Guilty, The Jury dismiss from their minds the plea of insanity altogether, but wish to recommend the prisoner to mercy on account of his youth.

Justice Channell turned to Walter Couzens and asked him if he had anything to say. The terrified youth tried to say No, but not a sound escaped his lips. The Justice donned his black cap:

The jury have convicted you of the crime of murder. You have already expressed your sorrow at what has happened, and I do not desire to prolong the painful position in which you find yourself. The jury have made a most natural recommendation to mercy on the ground of your youth. That will be forwarded to the authorities who have the power to deal with it, which I have not, and I am quite sure that it will receive the most attentive consideration. What the result of that consideration will be I have no authority to say, but I do know it will be attentively considered. You have taken the life of this young girl, as you have acknowledged, and for that there is only one sentence known to the law which it is my duty to pass on you.

Justice Channell proceeded to utter the dread words of the death sentence, and even his magisterial voice trembled with emotion as he recited '… and the Lord have mercy on your soul'.

Walter Couzens was later reprieved and sent to gaol for the rest of his natural life.

CHAPTER 11

The Welford Pastures Tragedy
1911
She had half a dozen massive wounds on her skull.

Welford Pastures, the land to the south of the river between Welford and Barton, was the scene of a most distressing murder in January 1911. The area is one of scattered farms and cottages in the rich farmland between the villages. It has always maintained a distinctly rural air of tranquillity, but on the 5th, a Thursday, this peaceful idyll was totally shattered.

William Robbins had a distinguished career in the army. He had been born in Lower Guiting, Oxfordshire, in 1867 and raised in the village until he was about twenty. He enlisted for a thirteen-year term in the British Army, serving first in the 1st Devonshire Regiment in Burmah and the Far East. He returned from there with a medal, and settled in Gosport as a military policeman. The settled life of a Red Cap was upset by the outbreak of war in South Africa and he was returned to active service at the front, serving under General Sir Redvers Buller. William had survived his thirteen years in military service in reasonable condition, although he had managed to get malaria and some form of ague. He also suffered from the occasional epileptic fit, something that affected several members of his family. His father had died in Winchcombe Union Workhouse from severe seizures. In October 1900 he received his discharge and returned to England. At first he moved to Birmingham to find work, and whilst there he joined a medical club in an effort to bring these fits under control.

William was not destined to spend long in the city. His brother, Charles, had stayed in Lower Guiting and worked on the land, marrying and raising his family. William's uncle had by now died in Gloucester Asylum because of his epilepsy and

Charles was taken there in January 1900 for a brief spell. In 1901 Charles was once again becoming ill and William returned to Lower Guiting to be with him. Charles used his last days of sanity to ask William to look after his wife Sarah Ann and his children. There was Edith Maria, Kate, Charles and Ernest. Charles had to be removed to Gloucester Asylum for treatment but it was little help and he returned home to die amongst his family.

William was true to his word and looked after his brother's family after his death. He took work at several farms as a carter and after five years the family settled at Welford Pastures. William had secured the position of carter on Mr Postlethwaite's farm and they all moved into a little cottage some hundred yards from the main farmhouse. Although William and Sarah had not officially married, they now had a child of their own, Violet. From 1906 life in the little cottage overlooking the fields settled down to a pleasant domestic routine. As Edith Maria grew up she obtained a position as domestic maid at the farm and the lads helped in the fields.

Welford Pastures, from the 1880s O S map. Courtesy of Ordnance Survey

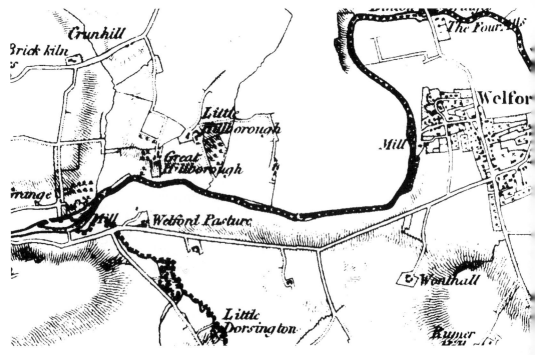

Their situation was by no means unusual. It was quite common for a brother to look after a widowed sister-in-law. This was an era with no effective social security and the survival of the children required Sarah Ann to find a reliable partner quickly. Love was a luxury that poor agricultural labourers could rarely afford.

By the spring of 1910 William began to suspect Sarah Ann was taking more interest in a neighbour than was seemly. Joseph Reeves used to come around to their cottage several evenings a week to play cards and join in the family sing songs. Reeves denied that there was anything going on but William constantly accused him and their cosy evenings of songs and cards ended. Reeves dared not visit the cottage whilst William was there. Sarah's son Ernest knew that he did call some days when William was out, but he said nothing. It would cause trouble.

Sarah Ann took to taking long walks in the country lanes each evening. This did little to allay William's suspicions about Reeves and he took him to one side in July, saying:

Do you know anything about my missus?

Reeves denied it and a sullen peace descended on the farmyard at Welford Pastures. Alfred Nicholls, who was William's assistant on the farm carts, knew all about the suspicions going through William's mind. Alfred himself was privy to most of what was going on in the Robbins' cottage as he had started walking out with their eldest daughter, Edith. This time William and Joe Reeves shook hands and parted amicably enough, but William later confided to Alfred that he still wasn't sure about Reeves, 'Reeves will have to alter his hand or there will be a row'. Sarah had been out until 9:00 the previous night, ostensibly with Edith, but Edith had been with Alfred.

The atmosphere had changed from domestic harmony to accusation and violence. It was too small a space for tempers to cool in private. In the one bedroom Sarah and the girls, Edith, Kate and Violet had to sleep on two beds whilst on the landing William, Ernest and Charles made do with mattresses on the floor.

Welford Pastures Farm viewed from the south. The farm was the central point in a small community of agricultural workers. The author

Early one July morning Ernest woke to hear a quarrel going on downstairs. William's voice was clear:

Where is the razor? I will cut your ——— throat.

Ernest raced downstairs to find his mother lying on the floor with William standing over her. He held an open cut-throat razor in his hand. Seeing Ernest, he quickly walked out of the kitchen and went up to the farm to work.

Sarah continued to see Joe Reeves out in the fields and on her walks to and from Bidford. Joe continued to deny anything was going on but ordinary friendship to William, but he was still deeply aggrieved. The harvest and the long days of back-breaking labour gave way to the shorter days of autumn. William told the ploughboy, William Hedges, 'I am a done man, all through Reeves'.

Ernest didn't know what to do. His uncle was becoming increasingly violent towards his mother, but not in his presence. Ernest, at eighteen years old, was a strong young man quite prepared to defend her. William wanted proof of Sarah's infidelity and threatened to cut her throat if he found it. He veered from aggressive to aggrieved moods. Ernest talked matters over with his mother and they agreed that it would be best for everyone if William was to move away. They managed to talk to him when he was in a compliant mood and he agreed to apply for jobs elsewhere with a view to moving out of their lives.

Christmas Day arrived and at lunchtime most of the farm workers walked down to the *Cottage of Content* for a drink with Mr Postlethwaite. William Robbins had far too much to drink, although Reeves, Nicholls and the others were not exactly sober either.

William walked back to his cottage with Ernest and Mr Postlethwaite. Mr Postlethwaite left them at the gate and returned to the farmhouse. As they walked into the kitchen William was muttering about getting his revenge. Ernest was heartily tired of this talk and asked him what he meant. He replied:

> *I have nothing to say against you, but I will have my revenge against that scamp Joe Reeves.*

He picked up a knife from the table and waved it around. Ernest told him to put it down as Sarah came into the room. She quietly observed that if William had anything to say to Joe, he was standing outside.

William rushed out of the cottage door and confronted Joe. Shouting abuse and waving his fists about he demanded to know what he was doing there. Joe replied he was doing nothing. William turned on Sarah, who had followed them out, and threatened to break her neck before he was done with her. He raced back into the cottage, grabbed his razor and emerged to attack Joe Reeves with this vicious blade. His drunken assault backfired as he slashed at Joe; the blade was turned back and sliced into his own fingers, cutting two of them to the bone. Ernest and Joe struggled to get the weapon off William before he did some serious damage. Losing the razor William grabbed a pitchfork from the washhouse and lunged madly at Joe.

Joe sidestepped the blow and the momentum of his thrust carried William and the pitchfork forward until the tines hit the ground, breaking one clean off. Dropping the pitchfork William now grabbed an ordinary garden fork and turned back for another lethal strike. Joe had picked up the pitchfork and fended off the shorter fork with ease. Panting with exertion the two men paused, William's homicidal rage was subsiding and the pain from his wounded hand finally penetrated his beer soaked mind. He dropped the fork and went into the kitchen. Outside Ernest and Joe exchanged puzzled looks as they heard William call for Joe to come in and have a drink so they could put matters right.

They went into the cottage and William had indeed got them a drink. After a few minutes William lay down on the sofa and fell fast asleep. It was clear to Joe and Sarah that something had to be done. Some sort of calm prevailed for the

Mr Robbins worked as a carter in these stables, looking after the horses and carts.
The author

next few days. William decided he would definitely leave and Sarah agreed that this would be the best course of action for all of them. On Boxing Day William apologised to Joe Reeves and said it was the fault of the beer.

On 4 January William got back from work and the family spent the evening talking and singing songs as though there was nothing amiss. William went to his bed at 8:30, Sarah and Edith followed an hour later. Ernest, sleeping on the landing, heard his uncle fetch a glass of water at about eleven, and the household fell silent as they all drifted off to sleep.

Long before dawn William Robbins quietly got himself dressed and went up the road to the farm. In the stables he busied himself grooming the three big plough horses, arranging their harness and tying up their tails in a bob so that they would be ready when the ploughboy arrived from his home at Crooked Cottage in Bidford. The farm was almost silent apart from the lowing of the cattle in the milking parlour where old Mr Hedges was doing the morning milking. For some reason William Robbins decided to return to his cottage once the horses were ready.

In the grey half-light of dawn William Hedges was walking along the road to work on the farm. His father had passed the same way some time earlier as he had to do the milking. William noticed William Robbins running across Holders Meadow towards the river. This was peculiar enough, but as he passed the Robbins' cottage at 6:30 he heard a strange groaning from behind the hedge. Deeply frightened he ran the rest of the way to the farm to find his father:

Dad, the carter was running up the meadow to the river and someone is groaning in the garden.

William Hedges senior was busy milking the last cow and told him he would have to finish that before he could come and look.

In the meantime Alfred Nicholls was also walking along the road. He too heard a groan from behind the hedge and went to investigate. He found Sarah lying on the garden path, surrounded by the washing she had been fetching off the line.

It was all splattered with blood, and Sarah was bleeding heavily about the head. He picked up her limp body and carried her into the kitchen and set her down on the floor. He shouted to wake someone but there was no reply. The house seemed empty. Alfred ran to the farm for help.

Alfred and William Hedges senior hurried back to the cottage. It still seemed empty so they went upstairs and managed to rouse Ernest. Alfred washed the blood from Sarah's face. She was unconscious and badly wounded about the head. Outside William found a large pool of blood on the path and a hatchet with traces of blood lying by the hedge. Before they had left the farm they had raised the alarm and Miss Postlethwaite had been sent to Bidford to fetch the doctor. Alfred stayed with Sarah while Ernest and William decided to search for Robbins.

They set off across Holders Meadow. There were bloodstains on the fence between them and the river. They found even more pools of blood on the grass of the riverbank and looking around, Ernest spotted Robbins' cap floating in the water. It seemed clear to them that William Robbins had finally snapped, tried to murder Sarah and had now thrown

Welford Pastures Farm Cottage was home to the whole Robbins family. It was just a few yards down the road from the main farm. The author

himself into the river to commit suicide. They returned to the little cottage. Ernest tried to talk to his mother, but as she drifted in and out of consciousness she only managed to say one word:

Don't.

Dr Crawford managed to get to the cottage by 8:00. He found Sarah lying on the sofa in a semi-conscious state. She had half a dozen massive wounds on the skull, shattering the bones like an egg shell. He surmised from their shape that she had been hit with the back of the hatchet. There were other marks on her ribs. She soon lapsed into a coma and by lunchtime was nearly dead. There was nothing the doctor could do for her, she died just after one o'clock surrounded by her children.

Unknown to Ernest and Alfred as they scooped William's hat out of the Avon, he had not drowned in the icy water but dragged himself out further downstream. At 8:40 PC Meade was standing on the doorstep of Long Marston police house when Miss Postlethwaite arrived. She had just begun telling him about the dreadful occurrence when he was astounded to see William Robbins stagger along the street and right up to him. He was wringing wet and blood was pouring from a ragged cut across his throat. He held a razor in his hand. PC Meade called for Sergeant Spragg to help and they got him inside and rubbed him down with warm towels. He was nearly dead from the cold and loss of blood. They managed to get him into a bed and William made the following statement:

I am a carter in the employ of Mr Postlethwaite of Welford Pasture and I returned home from South Africa about ten years ago. My brother requested that after his death I should look after his wife and children, which I did. I am not married to her but she has been co-habiting with Joseph Reeves at Welford Pastures. This morning I got up at five o'clock and went and saw to my horses. I then returned home to breakfast when I saw my woman and I hit her with a stick or a piece of iron, I don't know which. I have suffered from fits and this is the cause of this.

Dr Johnson of Mickleton arrived at the police house and decided that William needed to be transferred to Stratford Hospital. Superintendent Jones of the Stratford force had now arrived as well. He had been to the cottage and watched Sarah's life slowly ebbing away. William spoke to him:

Ah this is a bad job.
Yes, but you had better say nothing about it at present.
No, but if only you had been there to have stopped me. The feeling came over me and I felt bound to kill her.

Superintendent Jones drove William Robbins to Chipping Campden police station where he was formally charged with the wilful murder of Sarah Ann. He replied:

Well all I can say, Mr Jones, is I done it. I only wish to swing by the neck for it. I am guilty of what you charge me with. I killed the woman and I am sorry for it. She began it and I finished it. I don't think I can say any more than that.

The next week an inquest was opened. The jurors were taken by cart to see the little cottage; one of them nearly passed out and had to be revived out in the fresh air. It was small consolation that the chap was now on the very spot where Sarah was attacked. William remained in the hospital and the inquest was adjourned for a few days. Joseph Reeves flatly denied that there was anything between him and Sarah. Only one witness spoke of William suffering from any sort of epilepsy. George Massey had once found him staggering about in a dazed state in the rickyard; but no one else had ever known him have a fit. This included his nephew Ernest, who would surely have been in the best position to know him. The inquest proceeded in an orderly way up until Joe Reeves was called. Robbins jumped up and shouted:

I don't know that it is any good. He has told a lot of lies about the woman. He distinctly said, and the woman distinctly said that they had acted improperly. Did you or did you not?
No, I did not.

Well then, the woman was a liar. You were always going after her at night and that is what caused the grievance between us. It is no good you standing there telling barefaced lies.

The chairman told Robbins to keep calm, but he carried on:

No sooner had I gone back after tea than she has been out after him. I am sure that he has been there, so it is no good his telling lies. He is the cause of this crime and that is all about it. I have been along with Sir Redvers Buller and faced death before, and if the law holds me up I will face this out. It is not a morsel of good saying anything more. You are the cause of this crime on me, Joe. No I am not. Reeves shouted back.

William was committed for trial at Gloucester Assizes. It was a short trial. William was found to be insane; his family history was a major factor in the decision. He was committed to an asylum for the rest of his natural life. The only real surprise was that when Joseph Reeves was called to give evidence, he finally admitted that he did indeed have a relationship with Sarah.

CHAPTER 12

The Wootton Wawen Shooting
1913
She was dead before she hit the floor.

Harry Tomes was the despair of his ageing parents. At forty years old he was still single and still living at home. He worked as the village blacksmith in his father's forge at Wootton Wawen and also travelled the district attending to the horses on the many farms in the locality. His father, William, had long since stopped the arduous work of smith and earned his money as a carpenter; his mother, Emma, was fairly frail. Both of them were quietly terrified of Harry and would try not to antagonise him, particularly after he had been on the booze.

Outside of the house Harry was quite well liked. He had a cheerful manner and happily chattered away to everyone in the

The Bulls Head, *at the heart of the village, has witnessed some strange events over the years.* The author

small community. Through the summer of 1912 he was particularly friendly with the Chamberlain family who lived in the long old cottage near the *Bulls Head*. He got on well with Henry Chamberlain, often going for countryside rambles with him, and was often found in the cottage with Henry and his wife Clara and their two little boys. Henry was the carter for the local builder, Samuel Keyte. Clara had come to Wootton from her large family in Burton-on-Trent and was thirty-two that year.

In a small village there is little that goes unseen. By the end of the summer several people had noticed that Harry Tomes was visiting the Chamberlains' cottage rather more often when Henry was out than when he was at home. They kept their suspicions to themselves and Henry was completely unaware of Harry's visits. Harry's mother soon found out though, and told him it was not the right thing to do. Harry blew up and created such a scene at home that they feared to mention the subject again. The trouble was that Harry and Clara's relationship was becoming more noticeable.

On the Saturday before Christmas Emma Tomes met Harry and Clara walking down the road, bold as brass, holding hands. They broke their grip as she came close and she muttered to them that it was neither nice nor wise; but the couple simply walked on saying not a word. Later that day there was another family row in the Tomes' household and Harry decided he would move out for a while.

Harry returned to the village in the New Year, apparently reformed from his excessive drinking and got back to work as the village blacksmith. The gossip in the village remained muted and Henry Chamberlain was kept in the dark. Harry's new leaf didn't last long at all and soon he was back at the bottle, and back at the Chamberlains', especially when Henry was off on a long trip with his cart. His parents kept on at him about how unseemly this was, but simply received a tirade of abuse for their concern.

Sooner or later the truth would come out. Quite possibly Clara had decided that their secret meetings must stop before Henry discovered them. The village gossips would eventually tell Henry what was going on, out of sheer malice and jealousy if nothing else. There's nothing like a good scandal to keep a small community entertained. It can only be presumed that Harry, spoilt by his parents, had never been denied like this before. Outwardly he seemed normal enough, but inside he was boiling with rage.

It was Harry's 41st birthday on the 3 March. He got up as usual at 5:00 and left the house at 6:30 to go to Preston Hill Farm where Mr Philip Heller had some horses that needed some attention. The farm was a couple of miles away, and the work didn't take very long. By breakfast time Harry was in the *Crab Mill* sinking a couple of pints with the landlord William King Bazeley. He then returned to Wootton along the canal towpath and reached the *Navigation Inn* at 9:30. Harry was a regular at the *Navigation* and he spent an hour or so talking with the landlord Albert Boswell. Albert found him to be in a bright and chatty mood, slightly tipsy when he left, but by no means drunk.

Back in the village Dr William Nelson was in the Chamberlains' cottage to see how their son George was

Pound Cottage. No one will ever be truly certain of the relationship between Mrs Chamberlain and Harry Tomes. The author

getting on. George had been poorly over the weekend but now he seemed to be on the mend. Clara and Henry settled George into bed at 10.30 and walked up the road to the shop. Henry then went off to work and Clara back to the cottage to get on with the washing. She was far more cheerful now that the doctor had given the little seven-year-old a check up and said he would be alright.

Harry Tomes left the *Navigation* and walked to Field Farm at the other side of the village, across the fields from the back of the Chamberlains' cottage. At eleven o'clock he found Mr Boulton, the farmer:

Good morning Mr Boulton, I should like to borrow your gun as I want to shoot my dog. It has broken its leg and I want to put it out of its misery.

It seemed a reasonable enough request. Harry had a little terrier and the thought of it suffering with a broken leg was enough to convince Thomas Boulton to lend Harry his shotgun. Harry asked if he could have two cartridges just in case he missed because of nervousness. He said a man was apt to miss sometimes. When Thomas got the gun out, Harry asked for a bag to put it in since he no longer held a gun licence. Mr Boulton asked if he could be sure to bring the gun back later on as there were some rooks to be sorted out. Harry promised to bring it back at dinner time. Harry Tomes went off down the drive and Mr Boulton went back to his work.

Clara Chamberlain was getting on with the washing in the little outhouse at the back of the cottage. Young George was lying on the sofa in the front room with his younger brother. Whilst Clara was up to the elbows in soapsuds William Hedges arrived. He was the baker from Henley and he put the bread on the kitchen shelf and Clara paid him. He left the cottage at 11:45.

A few moments later little George was startled to hear someone swear loudly and suddenly in the washhouse. It wasn't his mother. Seconds later there was a deafening bang. Harry Tomes had appeared at the back door, his unexpected presence caused Clara to turn around and jump up. Before she even had time to raise her hands in defence he raised the shotgun and fired straight at her face. The charge blasted right through her jaw, through her brain, and blew out the back of her skull. She was dead before she hit the floor. Harry Tomes sat down beside her, put the muzzle of the gun below his right ear and pulled the trigger. The explosion blew off the right side of his head.

In the sudden silence George got off the sofa and went to see what had happened. He found his mother and Tomes lying on the floor. He went to hug his mother, but as he put his hand beneath her head he realised there was blood pouring out of the massive wound. Whimpering in terror he quickly put his clothes on and ran into the street. Fearing further horror he went back into the charnel house and grabbed his baby brother.

Joseph Keyte was by the Post Office when the little boy ran up to him, he was clutching his brother in bloodstained hands. George asked where his father was but Joseph had no idea. George then told him that his mother and Tomes were lying shot in the house. Samuel Keyte had now arrived and they went to the house to see for themselves. A truly ghastly spectacle awaited them. The walls and ceiling of the washhouse were splattered with blood and brains. Tomes lay with one leg across Clara on a floor soaked in blood.

The news quickly spread through the village. PC Archer was quickly on the scene. He found Tomes lying with the gun between his legs, and searching his pockets found that he was also carrying a cut-throat razor, another pair of shotgun cartridges, a knife and his pipe. It seems he was prepared for murder even if he hadn't managed to borrow the gun. Inspector Wright sent a telegram to Clara's family near Burton, and the bodies were removed to Henley mortuary. Clara's brothers immediately got on a train bound for Wootton, although at first they didn't know the exact reason for their urgent summons by the Inspector. As they passed through the stations at Birmingham it became all too clear. Newspaper placards gave the grim headlines.

For many people the events were inexplicable. Both the Chamberlains and Tomeses were well-respected local families of long standing. Few people knew of or suspected any liaison between Clara and Harry, indeed there may not have been one. Harry's parents seem to have been certain enough of it, but Henry Chamberlain couldn't believe it all, and completely broke down at the inquest. The only people who knew exactly what was happening were both dead.

Grave Robbery, 1830

Wootton Wawen was no stranger to dark deeds. Back in 1830 the supply of cadavers to medical institutions was haphazard and limited. The bodies of executed criminals were the only legal source of bodies for research, and despite the gory tales herein, they were in short supply. A certain amount of free enterprise made up the shortfall. Bodies that hadn't been overly stretched on a gallows commanded a premium and there were plenty of predatory characters just waiting for someone else's misfortune.

Joseph Oliver buried his wife in the churchyard at Wootton Wawen on 1 February 1830. Mary had died a couple of days before and despite his grief he took the precaution of paying a couple of sturdy men to keep watch on the grave each night.

The church at Wootton Wawen dates back to Saxon times when it was the principal church of a parish that extended for many miles. The author

Grave robbing was all too common in those days. The men kept guard in the churchyard for four nights.

During the last of these four days a rather foolish and stupid looking young man turned up in Henley and stayed in the *White Swan*. He bought a shovel in the town and returned to the *Swan* the following evening. An old man met him there and they went off on a cart drawn by a grey horse. They arrived at Wootton church in the dead of the night having picked up another shady character.

John Wichham, the rather daft looking youth who had bought the shovel, hurriedly dug up Mary Oliver's grave and pulled out her body. He gave a signal and the other two brought the cart close and they heaved the body into a bag, dumped it on the cart and drove off. Before they went they gave John Wichham fourteen shillings and left him standing in the road.

A couple of days later the staff at the *Bell* in Northfield were wondering what was in a box left with them. The box was

The scene of the grave robbery. The author

addressed to someone in London and had been brought there by an old man with a cart drawn by a grey horse. He called himself Mr Chambers. The local constable decided to open up the box, and found the body of Mary Oliver in it.

Word had got around quickly after the desecration of Wootton churchyard. Joseph Oliver travelled to Northfield to identify the body and ensure that it was returned for reburial. poor man must have been heartbroken. Perhaps it was remorse, but John Wichham then confessed to his part in the crime, saying he had met a Mr Chambers and Mr Grainger in Birmingham who had persuaded him to join them in the dark crime. He was sentenced to six months' hard labour.

CHAPTER 13

The Living Skeleton
1922
... she was covered in sores and fleas.

Before the National Health Service and before Social Services, if someone became seriously ill the choices were stark indeed. If illness was then combined with neglect you had all the ingredients of a horror story.

Elsie Chataway left her home in School Road, Alcester to become a domestic servant for Gertrude Harrison before the Great War. Elsie was only about twelve when she went into service. Her education hadn't been a great success; Mary Thursley, the schoolmistress, thought Elsie was a bit dull but had a sweet temperament. Elsie worked for Gertrude for the best part of six years before she was called home to help her mother.

The Chataway family consisted of Ellen and William, the parents, and their children, Elsie, Alfred, Nellie and William. Ellen stayed at home looking after the household whilst William worked as a drayman for the local brewery. Ellen was a proud woman and barely spoke to her neighbour, Kate Travis. The family kept themselves aloof from the rest of School Road.

Elsie was about nineteen and the year was 1916. She was a tall girl, 5'8", although slender. Her mother Ellen needed some help to look after the other children. Alfred was fifteen, Nellie, thirteen and William jnr, just eleven. Alfred intended to join the army, removing one of the older pairs of hands. Within a year Alfred had left and Nellie had finished school and gone into service, staying with her aunt whenever she was between posts. Elsie gave up her job and returned home to help her mother. The trouble was that she started to suffer from rheumatism in her hands and feet and spent increasing amounts of time in bed. This was an era of private medicine and calling out the doctor was an expensive business. It was an option denied to poorer families.

The months and years passed, Alfred returned from the war and found that his sister was now so ill that she rarely stirred from her bed. William jnr was living at home too. The two-bedroom house was divided such that Elsie and her mother shared one bedroom and the father and boys the other. Ellen undertook the nursing duties and the boys rarely saw their sister. Nellie came back for Christmas and was horrified to discover how ill her sister had become. She told her mother that the doctor should be called in regardless of the expense.

Ellen Chataway had by now entrenched herself in an impossible position. She was far too proud to call in the doctor and her nursing care of Elsie had been far from ideal. Elsie gradually weakened through 1920 and 1921, eating less and less, hardly stirring from her bed. Her two brothers and her father took no interest in her condition at all, simply relying on Ellen's word that she was poorly. William jnr occasionally heard her call good night but even these faint words tailed off through the winter of 1921. Ellen was now out of her depth, incapable of providing adequate care but still too proud to call in professional help. Elsie was trapped in a vicious circle, as she weakened her appetite faded and her mother finished off her meals for her. She gradually became emaciated and lacked the strength to get out of bed. Her mother stopped changing the sheets and discouraged her father and brothers from seeing her.

The neighbours knew something was wrong. Kate Travis, next door, hadn't seen Elsie for six years; but in 1921 there was no Social Services to investigate such a peculiar absence. Nellie came home at Christmas 1921 and berated her mother for neglecting Elsie. The bedroom was filthy and Elsie was lying on a bed infested with fleas; she hadn't been washed for months. Nellie didn't realise the full gravity of the situation.

After several years of trusting his wife's comments about his daughter, William Chataway happened to look into her bedroom on the afternoon of 3 May. He was utterly shocked to find his daughter at death's door. He immediately called in Dr Dorothy Alice Daley.

Ellen tried to cover up her negligence, carrying Elsie into the other bedroom and putting her on a clean sheet. Dr Daley was not deceived when she examined Elsie. She was covered in sores and fleas, her skin shrunken over her bones and discoloured. She asked William what the meaning of it all was, and he said he knew nothing, he had not seen Elsie for over six weeks. He appeared to the doctor to be completely dazed by the state of his daughter. He asked her if it was a hopeless case, and she told him that it was. His daughter could die that very night. Dr Daley insisted that Elsie was given milk and brandy in a last ditch attempt to revive her.

At the Infirmary Dr Daley and Dr Spencer discussed the case. Dr Daley had never seen such a serious case of neglect and was unsure of how to proceed. Did her oath of confidentiality prevent her contacting the police? They decided that it should not and sent word to PC Masters that he was needed. The two doctors then returned to School Road and the ailing Elsie.

Elsie was still conscious but incredibly weak. She was removed to the Infirmary. The doctors, realising that the filthy state of the girl did not match the bed she was lying on, insisted on searching the house. As soon as they entered the back bedroom they found a scene of utter squalor, a bed heaving with vermin and a pervasive stench. PC Masters joined them and was horrified at the ghastly conditions Elsie had been subjected to. It was doubly awful for him as he had known William Chataway for many years and always found him to be a decent hard-working chap. The sight of this filthy pit shocked him to the core. Elsie was a living skeleton.

Elsie gradually slipped away that night. She weighed just three stone thirteen pounds, her skin stretched taut over her bones. The doctors could do nothing to save her. The following day they called in a pathologist from Birmingham to do a post-mortem. His conclusion was that Elsie had been systematically starved to death over a period of years. No one could understand why Elsie had never once complained.

Ellen and William Chataway were sentenced to five years in prison each. Ellen because she had neglected her daughter and William because, as the master of his household, he should have controlled his wife.

CHAPTER 14

Murder on Meon Hill
1945
... a dark place on the edge of the valley.

One of Stratford's most famous murders is that of Charles Walton on the slopes of Meon Hill in 1945. The case remains open, an unsolved mystery behind a wall of sullen silence.

Meon Hill dominates the Avon Valley. Its brooding bulk overlooks the level fields closer to the river, visible for miles. The local saying goes 'If you can see Meon Hill it's going to rain, if you can't see it, then it is raining'. This dour reputation goes back thousands of years, as does its connection with witchcraft and the old ways. The murder of Charles Walton brought back the fear of these old superstitions; he was killed in what seemed to be a distinctly ritualistic way, on a particularly important date. The killing brought an air of ancient terror into a world that was just embracing rockets and radar.

The hill has stood there mute and sinister since before the arrival of mankind. On its crest are ditches and bumps, long weathered down, that are all that remain of its use before Rome was even built. As the Stone Age gave way to the Bronze Age the population increased and more land was brought into cultivation. These Stone Age peoples have left traces all around the district; long barrows dot the fertile plains along the Avon. Stone circles and menhirs were built in special places such as the Rollrights at the southern tip of the county. Whatever strange rites and magic these primitive peoples used have been lost to history.

Celtic civilisation expanded across Europe after 1000 BC. These people were skilled in the use of iron as well as the more traditional metals of copper, tin and gold. They arrived in this region somewhere around 700 BC and presumably mixed in

The hill above the village was a centre of an Iron Age society. The author

with the existing locals, bringing their new technologies and philosophy. It seems that the Bronze Age peoples lived a highly communal sort of life, with collective graves in long barrows. The Celts appear to have been far more individualistic, with a more stratified social hierarchy. Their Chieftains were buried alone in round barrows together with enough goods to see them through to the next life. The stone circles and long barrows lost their ritual uses but remained the source of legends.

Society around Stratford was centred on several agricultural settlements grouped around hill forts at Beausale near Warwick and at Meon Hill, and the route between these two crosses the Avon at Tiddington. Not surprisingly there are strong traces of an Iron Age agricultural village where this road crosses the one going north/south. This spot seems to be the very first settlement of what we now consider Stratford. Meon Hill became a focal point for their new religion and magic; it was not a residential settlement.

Stratford lies towards the northeastern edge of the territory of the *Dubunni* tribe. Two coins were found in the excavations of the settlement in Tiddington, one from the *Dubunni* tribe and one from the *Coritiani*. These suggest that shortly before the Romans arrived the region was a busy and thriving rural economy. The *Dubunni* were a tribe of Celts who appear to have lived in the region for several hundred years. This tribe appears to have evolved locally rather than moved in from the near continent. No doubt the advantages of Celtic civilisation appealed to the indigenous population so that there was a fair degree of intermarrying as well as conquest, until the Celts could truly be considered natives of the area. The area ruled by the *Dubunni* included most of the Severn and Avon valleys. Their capital is believed to have been at Cirencester.

The brooding bulk of Meon Hill shows the ditches of the Iron Age hill fort to this day. Its proximity to the boundary of the *Dubunni* territory appears to have been confirmed by a hoard of iron currency bars found by its defence ditch. Apparently these iron bars were usually stored near the edges of a tribe's land. Quite what the Meon hill fort was used for remains unknown, although there is plenty of speculation. The hill forts in Warwickshire show little sign that they were lived in by some chieftain, although the presence of a hoard of currency bars may indicate that they were used for storage of food and other valuables. This hoard was found in the nineteenth century and is the largest one ever found in Britain.

The region seems to have been a loose alliance of small communities vaguely loyal to a chieftain. Just to make things even more complicated, there wasn't always just one top chief. The earliest records suggest that around AD 1 the south of the region was ruled by Corio, and the north, our bit, by his brother, Bodvoc. They appear to be followed by Catti and Anted. The tribe seems to have gained a single chieftain, Eisu, around AD 30. It was Eisu who was in charge when the Romans invaded Britain.

Celtic resistance to the first Roman invasion by Julius Caesar was to be expected. There had been plenty of trading with the other Celtic tribes across Europe. Even in these far off days the English Channel was as much a highway for trade and travel as ever it was a barrier to invasion. The first Roman foray was a bit of a failure. Storms broke up some of Ceasar's ships, the locals were particularly hostile and anyway Caesar had an appointment back in Rome ... on the Ides of March. It all got a lot more serious when Claudius decided to have another go at subduing what was now one of the last bastions of Celtic religion and resistance.

Wherever you are in the village the hill is always present, looming on the horizon.
The author

Did Eisu and his druids stand atop a blood drenched, windswept Meon Hill shrieking dark curses at the invading Romans? Well no … they did a deal.

When the Roman legions conquered the local tribes the old rituals and beliefs gradually went underground or were absorbed into the Roman pantheon. Legends of Druidic sacrifices and fertility rituals entered our folklore, but the actual rites performed at sites like Meon Hill and the Rollright Stones were soon suppressed. Whether they completely vanished remains a moot point.

The cult of Epona survived. This was one of the Celtic goddesses who successfully fitted into the Roman pantheon. She looked after the tribe's horses and foals, and the Roman cavalry officers, so dependent on their horses, adopted the cult. No doubt other cults survived in a variety of new disguises. The fertility of the land was utterly crucial to survival and sacrifices of one sort or another were considered essential.

Of course the Romans eventually left, leaving the Avon Valley unprotected. The little village of Stratford fortified itself against the incursions of yet another wave of invaders from the east, the Anglo Saxons. From the summit of the hill the valley below became an empty and forlorn wilderness. The Romano British withdrew to fortified villages before the Saxon tribe of *Hwicca* settled the valley. They brought with them a variety of Germanic Gods and rituals. The *Hwicca* were one of the first tribes to convert to Christianity and the old gods were gradually marginalised. The Saxon tribes had some particularly unpleasant ways of sacrificing people to placate their gods. Hacking open the victim's chest to reveal the still beating heart being just one of them. Christianity was a definite improvement.

The Saxon villages gradually adopted Christian values and religion, encouraged by the later Norman invasion, but in an utterly static agricultural society older superstitions surrounding the fertility of the land were deep rooted. The centuries passed,

Lower Quinton Church today. The author

but the hill kept its air of mystery. Christianity very slowly permeated the villages around the hill, but older beliefs and superstitions lay dormant in the minds of the peasants and farmers. Christianity laid lightly over the countryside, old women with plenty of experience of childbirth became midwives, some men were considered wise in the ways of the seasons. Beliefs from thousands of years ago survived. Beliefs like how to kill a witch with a pitchfork. It must be said that sticking a pitchfork through someone's neck is going to kill them whether or not they are a witch, but it is supposed to stop the person creating any more trouble after they're dead, something for which witches are notorious. Local legend has it that John Haywood had said he would kill all sixteen witches in Long Compton, and set about the first with a pitchfork. Presumably he didn't get through all sixteen because of his arrest for the first. Another legend has it that a young man killed an old woman called Ann Turner in 1875 because she had bewitched him. Once again a pitchfork was the preferred weapon.

There are other superstitions, the sight of a black dog was considered very ominous. Not just any black dog of course, a spectral one. Local legend has it that Charles Walton met just such a dog when he was a young man. It passed him six days in a row, and on the seventh it turned into a headless woman. The following morning his sister died. This would certainly account for the man's dislike of black dogs but adds nothing to the theory that he himself was a witch. If so he would presumably have had some power over the dog as well as the ability to curse other people's corn and crops.

Seasons passed in their endless cycle of planting and harvest. The Second World War saw the arrival of bomber bases all along the Avon Valley, and the Army Camp at the foot of the hill had become a holding camp for prisoners of war. Charles lived in his little cottage in the village with his niece Edith. He was now seventy-four years old and suffering from arthritis, using a walking stick, but still capable of doing odd jobs on the local farms. He lived a frugal life, with a few savings in his Post Office Savings Account. By all accounts he was a well-respected and well-liked member of the village community.

February 14th 1945 saw him setting off to work on a hedge at Hill Ground on the slopes of Meon Hill. He had been laying a hedge there for some days and had been working on the farm for about nine months. He didn't have any set hours, but usually knocked off at teatime. Mr Alfred Potter, the manager of Firs Farm, paid him 1s 6d an hour, relying on Charles to tell him how many hours he had worked. Mr Potter never had any reason to doubt that Charles had indeed worked the hours he claimed. Charles went off to the hill without seeing anyone.

At midday Mr Potter and Mr Stanley left the *College Arms* to look at Mr Stanley's broken down tractor. Alfred Potter then walked up to the hill with some feed for his cattle and check the sheep. He looked over towards where Charles was working. He saw a man in shirtsleeves and presumed that it was Charles Walton. He returned to the farm and got on with the usual rounds of jobs, pulping mangolds, dragging a heifer out of a ditch with another farm hand, Mr Batchelor.

Edith Walton returned from work at 6 o'clock. Her uncle was not in the cottage, and clearly had not returned from

The small community closed ranks against the intrusion of Inspector Fabian of Scotland Yard. To this day the murder remains unsolved. The author

work. She was concerned that he may have fallen and went round to her neighbour Mrs Beasley. Edith and Harry Beasley looked around the fields close to the village but found nothing. Together they went to see Mr Potter to see if he knew where he might be. Mrs Beasley went back to the cottage whilst Edith, together with Mr Potter and Harry Beasley set off up the hill to find out what had happened to Charles.

The two men were in front of Edith when they arrived at the hedge. Harry Beasley could see that Charles was in a terrible state, and stopped Edith going any further. Mr Potter yelled to Mr Peachey in the next field to go and call the police. Harry Beasley took Edith back to the cottage. Mr Potter remained with the body, picking up the trouncing hook that had been used.

Charles Walton had been killed in a most violent manner. He had tried to defend himself with his walking stick, but had received three massive blows to his chest with the hook, smashing his ribs, the hook left embedded in his chest on the last blow. He had fallen over in the frenzied attack. He had then been stabbed through the neck with his pitchfork, cutting open all the arteries and pinning his now lifeless body to the hillside. His attacker then searched his pockets, and vanished.

PC Lomasney arrived shortly after the gruesome discovery. He confirmed that Charles was dead and noticed that his braces had been broken at the back, but unbuttoned at the front. He also noticed that Charles's watch chain was in his waistcoat, but the watch was not attached to it. There was no money left in his pockets.

The sheer horror of the attack staggered everyone. The county police force became involved immediately and before midnight Professor J. Webster from the Forensic Science Laboratory was examining the body in situ, taking photographs and gathering any clues possible. Superintendent Alec Spooner was called in from Warwick and realised that this was so utterly unlike any normal murder, that he placed a call to Scotland Yard for assistance. This was no common domestic argument, there was something deeper; if there was a maniac on the loose he must be caught urgently.

Inspector Fabian of Scotland Yard and his assistant, Sergeant Webb, arrived in the village before dawn. Superintendent Spooner led them up to the bloodstained hedgerow. He may already have had his suspicions about the case because when Fabian asked about the possible motive, he gave him a couple of books detailing the witchcraft murders of Warwickshire. Sergeant Webb was dismissive of such superstitious twaddle, but Alec Spooner said 'You wait and see, my lad'.

The ancient bulk of Meon Hill was subjected to the entire arsenal of modern forensic science. Inspector Fabian had resources beyond the ordinary County Police and by mid afternoon an RAF Anson plane was circling overhead taking detailed photographs, platoons of soldiers were using mine detectors to scour every inch of the fields and footpaths, spotting footprints in the mud, hunting for that missing watch. All they found were some rabbit snares.

The prisoner-of-war camp at Long Marston was only a couple of miles away, and not exactly the height of security. John Messer, the local baker, had seen one of the internees lurking in a ditch near the hill, wiping blood from his hands. An interpreter was summoned and all the 1,043 prisoners interviewed. Several of them soon pointed an accusing finger at one of the Italians. They had seen him washing blood off his coat. Inspector Fabian rushed the coat off to the lab for analysis, confident that they had their man.

The following day the Italian's story was vindicated; it was rabbit blood. He had set the snares to supplement the dull diet of the camp. That just left the 500 residents of the locality to interview. This got him precisely nowhere. Fabian had taken casts of every single footprint found on the hillside, and traced every one to its owner. No small feat in itself, but once again he drew a blank. As the weeks passed he became less and less confident of catching the murderer. If he walked into the *College Arms* it went silent. His enquiries started to be met with answers like 'he's dead and buried now, what are you worrying about?'.

Inspector Fabian returned to London, his investigations stalled amid walls of silence. The case naturally remains open. What really did happen?

Meon Hill remains a dark place on the edge of the valley, its air of eldritch silence enhanced by the mysterious murder. Did Charles Walton really die in some satanic ritual designed to improve the fertility of the land by spilling human blood into the soil; was he hacked down to stop a black magic curse rotting the crops in the fields? It could be that he was simply smashed down by some itinerant maniac or escaped prisoner and robbed for the loose change in his pockets. There is always the possibility that he disturbed a courting couple enjoying Valentine's Day in true country style, and threatened to expose the matter to their respective spouses. Only the hill knows for sure.

Chapter 15

A Difficult Year
1945
... yet another body was revealed in the mud ...

These days do-it-yourself has been elevated to a leisure activity, but it hasn't always been like this, and for some very good reasons.

Thomas William Brown had lived to a great age, but at ninety-three he was starting to drift away to that unknown land from whence there is no return. He was concerned that his daughter, Mary Jane, would be impoverished by all the expense of a funeral. He didn't like formal black jackets and piles of flowers; a simple cremation would do for him.

In early December 1945 he was ailing fast, Mary Jane propped him up in the kitchen chair and fed him tea out of a brandy bottle, he was too weak to hold a cup any more. He quietly whispered to her, 'Ah, you won't have a father much longer', leant forward and died. Mary Jane sat with him for a while and then decided to carry out his dying wishes.

A week later Mary Jane Brown was in serious trouble. Accused by the coroner of failing to provide her father with a Christian burial, she was taken from her home at The Heath, Kings Coughton, to stand trial at Alcester Magistrates' Court. The police were busy digging up the garden, but she was quite right when she said 'You'll never find him'. The Coroner and County Pathologist were hopping mad, they needed to find a cause of death to complete their paperwork, and there wasn't much to examine.

After Thomas died, Mary Jane had gone out into the garden and built a bonfire. Then using all her strength, she was sixty-five after all, she dragged his body onto the fire and lit it. This was only partly effective, and so she spent the next three hours digging a large hole in the garden to bury what was left. She had to use a rope to drag the body off the fire and into the hole. It seems probable that the hole wasn't quite big enough. Some work with a chopper and double edged pruning saw was involved at this point.

Mary's sister did not approve of this course of action when she found out.

The police arrived and started to dig up the garden, but Mary had done her work thoroughly, and they only found Thomas's torso. She was indignant at their intervention, what business of theirs was it?

Professor Webster gave his opinion; he could not provide a cause of death because the head and neck were missing, so too were the arms and legs for that matter. Mary Jane was resolute in her defence stating that she was only carrying out her father's dying wishes:

> *I did that because I wanted to carry out his wishes … I put him in the hole and covered him up with earth … it took me three hours you know.*

The floodgate beside the old mill could be raised to lower the river level. On several occasions as the water fell, a scene of real horror was revealed. The author

1945 had been a pretty horrible year for the coroner. On 15 March the floodgates at Lucy's mill had been opened so that they could be cleaned and repaired. This dropped the level of water in the river so that it was just a trickle down the middle. A soldier had gone missing the day before, but no one had raised any serious alarm as yet. Soldiers were frequently late back to the camp and there were thousands in the various camps around the district, keeping track of them all was tricky.

Also missing was Mrs Annie Louisa Stayt. She had simply vanished from her home at 4 Ely Cottages on 16 December 1944, taking a bottle of whisky with her. She was eight months pregnant.

Mr F W Pope wound up the floodgates early in the morning and the water levels started to drop. At lunchtime he was looking down at the water swirling through the gap when he noticed something odd. As the water dropped it revealed a ghastly sight, the body of a woman was wedged against the gate. He called for help and PC Turner arrived, but as the water levels fell further yet another body was revealed in the mud opposite the church. PC Harris waded out across the riverbed to recover it.

Mr Archibald Roland Stayt had spent months worrying. He had taken Annie her breakfast in bed on the morning of 16 December before going to work. The pregnancy was going fine according to Dr Rees and Annie had been making preparations for the arrival. She was worried about having the baby from time to time, but so is every mother and her worries hadn't caused any alarm, not even when she once said 'I feel like jumping in the river.' Archibald thought it was a joke. Annie was seriously worried though, and with good reason. Her own mother had died in childbirth. Dr Rees had tried to calm her down and assure her that modern childbirth was much safer. Annie was thirty-eight years old, which was considered elderly for a first pregnancy at the time. Annie remained deeply apprehensive.

Archibald got back to the cottage at 1:30 on the 16th, and Annie was gone. He checked with the neighbours, called the police, but day after day, week after week, there was nothing but silence in the little house. Mid-January passed, without the expected arrival of the baby, with no news of Annie.

A grim Mr Stayt identified his wife's body by the boots and dress, and the distinctive whisky bottle that was still in her pocket. After three months in the river that was about all that could be done. Dr Rees attempted to discern the cause of the death but failed. Mr Lodder, the coroner, decided that Annie had taken her own life whilst of unsound mind. He turned to Dr Harold Rees and said 'You have had a very nasty job and done it well'. Dr Rees replied sadly, 'I think it was the worst in my experience'.

The identification of the second body was more straight-forward. He carried ID tags that proved him to be Private Thomas McKay from Airdrie in Scotland and he had been staying at the soldiers' camp to the south of the town. The previous Saturday night he had come into the town with a bunch of his mates and they had toured the town, starting at the *Horse and Jockey*, on to the *Green Dragon*, via the *Oddfellows* and ended up in the *Plymouth Arms*. His friends Robert and Desmond Murray decided that he had had more than enough to drink by 9:15. They left him at the *Plymouth Arms*, expecting to see him on the train back to the camp at 10:20. When he didn't show up at the station they thought he would be catching the 11:00 train, and anyway, even if he had spent all his money and couldn't afford the ticket, there was still the lorry waiting at the police station to round up the stragglers and take them back. It seems that Private McKay missed all of these, and never having been in trouble before, decided to walk back. Somehow he seems to have missed his way and fallen in the river; with a skinful of beer he stood little chance in the cold water.

CHAPTER 16

The Killing of Olive Bennet
1954
The assailant had then thrown her like a broken doll into the river ...

Stratford-upon-Avon has always been a magnet for people. Over the generations thousands have visited the town and ended up living here. The friendly atmosphere and the glorious variety of tourists from all over the globe, contributes to a cosmopolitan character quite unlike other small market towns. The mix of high art at the theatre, with its mildly eccentric actors, rural farmers, and industrial workers is completely unique. People arrive here and end up staying for the rest of their lives. In the case of Olive Bennet this turned out to be very brief indeed.

Olive was a diminutive midwife from Edinburgh. She arrived in Stratford in March 1954 and started work at the Monroe Devis maternity home in Tiddington. She had worked in many other hospitals over the years. Her training started in an era when nurses were expected to remain single and behave like nuns. The advent of the National Health Service after the war loosened things a little, but at forty-five years old she seemed to be a typical nurse; very prim and proper, cheerful with her patients and quietly religious. Naturally her vocation as a nurse meant that she had never married and led something of a cloistered and institutionalised life.

It was shortly after she moved from Bristol to Malvern that something changed in her personality. She had all her teeth removed in an operation at a local hospital and this seemed to trigger a complete alteration in her character. Perhaps it was a distinct reminder that the years were creeping up on her and she had, as yet, not had much fun in life. By the time she moved to Stratford she was living an almost schizophrenic lifestyle, cheerful prim nurse by day, and a sherry swilling,

Olive became well known in local hotels such as the Red Horse Hotel. Author's collection

chain smoking, bar-fly by night. She was subject to bouts of depression and rarely talked intimately with her fellow nurses.

Within a few weeks of her arrival Olive had become well known in most of the hotels. She had had several relationships with married men and the taxi drivers frequently took her back to the Monroe Devis in the early hours of the morning. Although she was having dozens of casual encounters with both locals and tourists alike, she confided in Sister Ann Swarbrick at the Monroe that she had a boyfriend. Ann could not be certain about who this man was however. Olive returned very late one night, freezing cold, and said she had been in the river. Another night she said, '... he must love me very much, because when he gets back to Stratford he has another four miles to walk'. Whether this boyfriend really existed remains in doubt, he could have been a convenient fiction to hide the fact that Olive was steadily working her way through most of the interested men in the town.

She was busy chatting with Mr Inglis in the local pub in Tiddington on Thursday 22 April. She ordered a sherry, 'Aren't I a naughty girl? I've had five already'. She was chain smoking throughout their conversation and she admitted to spending £200 on drink in the last eight months, but she had

'had a lot of worry'. One of the worries was probably her father's reaction to the money she was drawing out of her account. Another was that he was deeply suspicious of her apparent relationship with a middle aged man. In the five weeks that she had been in Stratford she had written to him regularly, full of praise for the town and the nurses at the Monroe. It seems that she had found the petty jealousies of her previous posting difficult to deal with. The atmosphere at the Monroe was much friendlier.

23rd April is always a special day in Stratford. The Bard's birthday celebrations, St George's Day, processions, parades and flags. The town is thronged with tourists, ambassadors, and cultural attachés. Olive and Ann had to stay at work during the day; babies aren't bothered by all that stuff and will insist on being born regardless. At 8:10 Olive seemed very cheerful and told Ann she was going into town to see her boyfriend and would be back at 2:00 am. Clarice Heggs, the cook, also saw her go out in a happy mood. She was wearing a brown velour Halo style hat, dark grey and white striped whipcord coat, brown shoes and was carrying a double strapped black box style handbag.

Olive arrived at the *Red Horse Hotel* in Bridge Street at about 9:00. This matches the time it takes to walk from Tiddington. Charles Ernest Waller, the night porter, saw her briefly and it seems she went off quite soon. The town was heaving with visitors to the Birthday Celebrations. There was even a television crew from the BBC filming an edition of *About Britain* and the theatre had a special performance on. Olive disappeared into the melee only to be seen again in one of the hotels at about closing time. Charles Waller saw her standing alone outside the hotel at 11:45. At about midnight the waiter from the *Avonside Hotel* saw a couple embracing beside the churchyard wall, and felt certain that the woman was Olive Bennet. It was the last time anyone saw her alive.

The next day Mr Thomas Anderson was tidying up the churchyard when he found a lower set of dentures, then a pair of spectacles, and then a brown shoe. They were scattered along the edge of the wall by the river. Somewhat concerned at this strangely sinister collection he called the police. They

The scene of Olive Bennet's final and fatal struggle with an unknown attacker. The author

started to search along the river's edge and found a black box style handbag in the water. The contents revealed it was Olive's. Fearing that she had committed suicide they proceeded to drag the river, throwing out a grappling hook and dragging it back. It took seven hours to get a grip on the body and pull it free. Something seemed to be holding the body down.

Although they assumed Olive had committed suicide, the county pathologist was called and found that she had extensive bruising around her neck. The cause of death was not drowning but strangulation. Worse still, it looked as though something had been used to sink her body. Another search of the graveyard revealed a missing tombstone. The floodgates of the river were drawn up so that the riverbed could be searched. A few hours later the tombstone was recovered.

Sometime in the night Olive Bennet had been fighting with someone. She lost her lower set of teeth in the fight and sustained multiple bruises; she was then throttled, her attacker repeatedly crushing her thin neck. The assailant had then thrown her like a broken doll into the river, wrenched up a gravestone and hurled it onto her floating corpse to sink it. Who this unknown person was, and why the sudden violence remained to be discovered.

The County Police were involved straight away. Olive's father, John Fraser Bennet, came down from Edinburgh to identify the body and give what information he knew. It soon became apparent that there was not so much a shortage of suspects, but a positive glut of them. Inside Olive's handbag was a diary, the existence of which sent a shiver of fear down many a respectable citizen. The sheer number of contacts meant that Superintendent Spooner asked for assistance from Scotland Yard. Detective Superintendent John Capstick and Detective Sergeant Heddon were sent to help.

The first person the police needed to trace was the man seen embracing Olive close to the churchyard at midnight. He was described as 5′10″ tall, middle aged and sturdy, with bushy fair

Olive's false teeth and other possessions were found scattered about the graveyard the following morning, leading to a search of the river. The author

hair. He was also wearing a gaberdine belted raincoat. It wasn't a great deal to go on. Interviews with Olive's friends at the hospital led them to believe that the man might be the mysterious un-named boyfriend who had to walk four miles from Stratford to get home. Within this radius were several army camps and they started to check the whereabouts of all their inmates. Whispers and rumours raced around Stratford. Several people came forward to help the police with what little information they knew. The trouble was that Olive had only recently moved to the town and most of her new friends had very good reasons to keep quiet about knowing her.

A coroner's inquest was opened and immediately adjourned on the following Wednesday. The post-mortem evidence was not presented but held back until the full inquest set for 30 June. The inquest did provide permission for Olive Bennet to be buried and her funeral took place at Alveston Church on Thursday 29 April. Olive's parents, the staff of the Monroe Devis and the detectives attended. The detectives were keen to see if any of Olive's acquaintances turned up. They didn't. Her room in the hospital provided a few letters and other personal items, but nothing to point an accusing finger of suspicion.

The following day, Friday, exactly a week after the murder, the police decided to hold a re-enactment of Olive's last known movements in the hope that it might trigger memories. It was not an easy task because Olive was so small. None of the policewomen in Warwickshire were anywhere near small enough to fit into her coat and eventually one of the typists at the *Stratford Herald* was co-opted for the task. Even then a tailor had to extensively alter the dress. The re-enactment produced little in the way of evidence. One person remembered seeing a couple of bicycles propped up against the churchyard wall, which possibly meant that there was another couple in the yard at the time of the murder. It could have meant anything really, the town had so many visitors that day that they could have been in the theatre, a hotel, anywhere.

As the re-enactment took place between Bridge Street and the church, police checkpoints were set up on Clopton and

Tramway Bridges; every pedestrian and motorist was interviewed for information. Another team of officers visited every hotel in the town, examining the visitor books searching with any clue, no matter how trivial. The military police had been busy interviewing the hundreds of soldiers billeted in the district.

By the next Wednesday the police had about a dozen men for whom they weren't entirely happy. An identity parade was arranged at Stratford Police Station to see if any of them matched the bushy haired man last seen with Olive. None of them did. In the meantime a name had surfaced as a possible suspect, and the Detective John Capstick together with Detective Inspector Eric Jenkins, flew to Ireland incognito. They gave their names as Mr Smith and Mr Brown and their address was one in Solihull belonging to the Chief Constable. They reported to the Garda in Dublin and then drove off to County Mayo and other undisclosed destinations.

At the Monroe Devis a letter arrived for Miss Bennet. It had been held up in the post, having originally been sent to her previous employer and then redirected. The letter was very brief, a simple confirmation of an existing appointment to meet her on 24 March. It was signed 'Harry'.

The police already knew of four men called Harry who knew Olive, but none of these had handwriting like that on the letter, and they all denied writing it. It was yet another clue that seemed to point nowhere. The house-to-house enquiries were proving just as fruitless. In the army camps the military police were checking each and every soldier with a somewhat more brusque approach to their questioning.

Once again the river was drained down, although the heavy rain of the previous week meant that the levels failed to drop as much as was hoped. Nevertheless they managed to recover Olive's other shoe, and some of the things that fell from her handbag during the struggle, a powder compact, a fountain pen, and other small items; nothing that shed further light on the identity of her killer. The forensic examination of the gravestone revealed nothing more than it weighed three-quarters of a hundredweight. This in itself meant they were looking for someone with sufficient strength to hurl a substantial block of stone several yards. It confirmed the opinion that the killer was a sturdily built man.

Detective Capstick returned from Ireland with no new information, and although the patient house-to-house enquiries were gradually extended to encompass the entire town, little more could be added. He was certain that there were several men in the town who had known Olive intimately, and although probably not guilty of the murder, may well have information that could lead to the man. By the third week of May he appealed for any of these men to come forward in absolute secrecy, even offering to meet them in a different town.

One small detail emerged that week, a man had been seen trying to hitch a lift out of town early on the Saturday morning. He had looked worried whilst he was eating breakfast in a transport café and was then seen trying to hitch-hike south. John Capstick travelled up to Lancashire to interview various members of a coach party who had seen him. He definitely wanted to interview this man.

The appeal for confidential interviews with Olive's lovers bore some fruit. One of them arranged a meeting in Staffordshire and provided a few more snippets of information. The hitchhiker going south had not been traced, but now there was another man to be found, one that fitted the description more accurately. The man going south was described as working class, and wearing no coat, whilst a man wearing a similar coat and matching the description had been seen walking along the Warwick Road in the middle of the night. It also transpired that Olive had spent some of the evening in the company of a couple of American tourists, a mother and daughter from Tennessee.

Detective Capstick had now drawn up a picture of Olive's movements from the day she arrived in town to within an hour of her murder. There were a few pieces missing from this jigsaw but on the whole he had discovered almost everything apart from the murderer. He had managed to avoid a scandal within the town as well. There were still plenty of people who were withholding information. Marriages and social standing were at risk from an admission of a relationship with Olive.

John Capstick wanted these people to come forward, in confidence if necessary, but if they wouldn't do so voluntarily he was prepared to put some pressure on them.

The detectives managed to track down one man mentioned several times in connection with Olive Bennet. He had left Stratford very quietly around the time of the murder and had apparently vanished. On 10 June they tracked him down to Southampton. He was just about to board a ship. Deeply suspicious, Bill Heddon interviewed him for hours. He managed to convince Detective Sergeant Heddon of his innocence; that he had left the town some hours before the murder. He gave what information he could to the police, and was allowed to board his ship just minutes before it sailed.

The following week a fragment of another letter turned up, but with no envelope or even the first two pages, only the handwriting and the tantalising name Harry could have any bearing on the case. The Scotland Yard detectives had interviewed a man in Nottingham and thought that they may have a concrete lead in Carmarthen. It was from this small Welsh town that the first letter had been posted. It was yet another failure. Despite scouring the visitor books for the hotels for the days when the letter was posted, nothing came to light. The trial was getting colder every day.

The Scotland Yard detectives could not stay on the case indefinitely. At the start of July they were needed back in London and in the absence of any new evidence, the case was left with the Warwickshire Police. They just had to hope that something would turn up. It didn't.

The months passed and the emotional cost mounted up. Names were anonymously sent to the police, every one requiring investigation. Some of these were indeed people who had had a relationship with the little midwife, others were just plain malicious. Detective Superintendent Spooner now had a lorry load of paperwork, none of which provided the slightest hint as to the identity of the killer. More worryingly, another murder, that of Jean Townsend in South Ruislip, bore some uncanny similarities.

Children in the town started to have nightmares about the still and now sinister waters beside the church. One of the soldiers who knew Olive found his life disintegrating. Sergeant Robert Williams had been seen speaking to Olive on the Thursday before her death. The military and then civilian police interviewed him twice a day for two months. He was even put into the cells for three days. He lost a stone in weight and was on the verge of a nervous breakdown by the end of the interrogation. His release failed to bring an end to his problems as the rest of his squad persisted in taunting him about being the murderer. He may well have been very relieved to be transferred to Saighton Camp near Chester. It was a short lived respite, Sergeant Standen was also transferred there and continued to harass him; getting him demoted to Corporal. The bad blood between them continued until Williams punched him to the ground. Striking a superior officer was a grave offence and Williams was reduced to the ranks. He was just one more person who wished that he had never heard of Olive Bennet.

CHAPTER 17

Foul Deeds and Suspicious Deaths on the Canal c.1816–1860
1843
It didn't take long for the boatmen to make their presence felt.

One of my pet topics is the canal. I've even written a book (*Stratford Canal*, Tempus, 2002) about it and like most books of its sort it covers the Industrial Revolution, architecture and cargoes, but little in the way of social history. This omission can now be remedied. The Stratford upon Avon Canal opened in 1816 and had an immediate impact, for example, with the reduction in the price of coal. From the local constables point of view it wasn't all roses though as it created lots more work! The town had been relatively peaceful, with a population of just over 2,000 and

It is hard to believe today, but the canal basin and Waterside were once the docks of the town. A maze of warehouses and stables served the canal and tramway. The area became a run down slum by 1880 as the traffic moved onto the new railways.
Ordnance Survey 1885

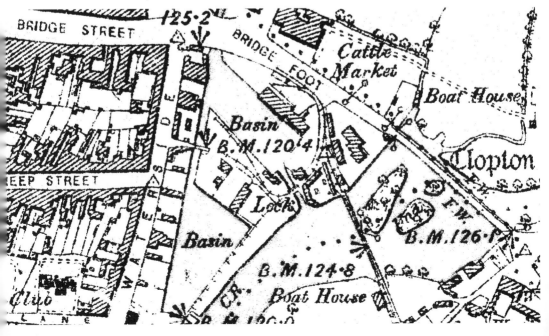

approximately 750 tourists a year; it was simple to keep a watchful eye on things. Suddenly there were strangers and new opportunities for crime and disorder.

It didn't take long for the boatmen to make their presence felt. On 20 January 1821 Marie McKine swore that William Heritage, a boatman, was the father of the child she was expecting. It wasn't unusual to find single women getting pregnant and accusing someone or other; the Petty Sessions are full of these cases. The woman was likely to be confined to the workhouse if she could not get support and this was a truly ghastly fate. Either later boatmen were less promiscuous or had fewer relationships with girls on the bank since this is the only case involving a boatman.

A good few altercations appear in the records, the bargees reputation for ferocious fights establishing itself early on. Richard Rogers and Thomas Sydney were at each other's

Lock 54 between the Maidenhead and Warwick Roads where Phoebe Tallis had to maintain order amongst the impatient boatmen, often at considerable risk to herself. The cottage and adjoining land was the canal company's carpentry workshop. Author's collection

throats in April 1824, both of them boatmen from outside the parish. It wasn't just the boatmen either. Phoebe, wife of the town's lock-keeper, John Tallis, had to stand up for herself when she found Joseph Lee jumping the queue and stealing a lock full of water. This was no joke since he managed to strand four boats aground in the process. During Lee's trial before the magistrate, Reverend Davenport, she swore, 'He called me for everything and then came and held his fist in my face and said he would mark me that I should carry it to the grave.' Joseph Lee got very short shrift from the magistrate, suffering a 40 shillings fine. I wonder if it was the assault on a woman or stealing the lock that was the worse offence? The Reverend Davenport was a major shareholder of the canal.

If fights involving lock keepers were infrequent, what went on in the three pubs beside the canal basin was bordering on anarchy. The pubs were *The Wheatsheaf*, *The Ship* and *The Anchor*. *The Ship* rapidly gained a reputation as a 'disorderly house', in other words a brothel. One girl's paternity claim was thrown out simply because she had been seen in *The Ship* and

The Warwick Tavern *was built by the local lock keeper John Tallis in 1831. It soon earned a reputation for bar room brawls. The boatmen were renowned for their hard drinking and rough lifestyle.* Author's collection

was thus considered a prostitute on that evidence alone. The Anchor was noted for rumbustious fights. John Tallis had built the *Warwick Tavern* specifically to cater for the boatmen's needs. It had extensive stabling for the horses and being just below Lock 55 was convenient for the town centre. It was right beside one of the boat-builders' yards too. It wasn't long before this was a regular stop on the constables' rounds.

Stratfords's main boat-builder during that decade, Samuel Monk, had something of a scrap with his senior apprentice Richard Beesley and had him charged with disorderly conduct in 1839. After this affair, incidents involving the canal diminish in the records, possibly because they all became reformed characters but more probably because the numbers of people involved with the canal started to decline.

The boatmen developed something of a reputation for being a little light-fingered where cargoes were concerned. It doesn't come as much of a surprise to find William Houghton helping himself to coal off a boat in 1826. The cases do provide an insight into the miscellaneous cargoes on the boats. In 1849 John Pargiter was charged with stealing cloth from a boat and Charles, alias Morgan, Houghton (a familiar surname) was accused of stealing the bed boards and table drawer off Edward Paine's boat. One long established cargo was glucose chips, brought to the industrial chemists Kendal's. In an era where sweets were rare for the poor, the boatmen regularly traded these lumps of pure sugar in return for just about anything. The boats were followed by gangs of children begging for lumps of the 'chemical'. Officially the sugar was destined to make the brewing syrup for Flowers Beers.

You would be tempted to think that anything would be stolen if it wasn't nailed down.; but not even that helped! Believe it or not, in 1828 Joseph Hanson and Thomas Huckrick were charged with stealing the sill off a lock gate on the Avon Navigation. How on earth they managed that I shudder to think; the sill is a large elm beam set into the bottom of the lock chamber some five feet below the water!

As the years progress towards the decline of the canal the nature of the thefts change. The last big heist was a load of rope from Samuel Monk in 1851. His boat-building trade was now in decline even though the railways had yet to reach the town. The boatmen were gradually being pushed into an economic corner. In 1853 the boatman Samuel Smith was charged with stealing corn from the mill and in 1856 Thomas Brain stole five chickens from Thomas King's farm.

The canal was a hazard for the locals as well, claiming its first drowned victim, Joseph Jesson, on 29 September 1833. The following year Phoebe Canning was going home after a few Saturday night drinks and slipped into the basin. Despite being pulled out after only a few minutes by a passer-by, she had drowned. It looks as though she tried to take a short cut across the lock gates and slipped. The year 1837 saw two more locals drowned in the canal near to the town centre. In 1858 Stratford was experiencing a hard economic recession and it was in this year that no less than three newborn babies were found drowned in the canal; their little lives cut short before they were even christened.

The boatmen faced far worse dangers than the town's constable. It was a hazardous job in a dangerous environment as the coroners' inquests bear out. Working boats in the winter

The canal by the Warwick Road was the scene of some grisly discoveries in the nineteenth century when no less than three newborn babies were found drowned. Author's collection

is a particularly tricky business. The only two industrial accident fatalities in the Stratford coroner's inquest reports took place in the bitterly cold winter of 1840-41. In December 1840 temperatures plunged and on the 30th Philip Parsley, aged only fifteen, slipped and fell between two boats at Wilmcote. This section of the canal was where the limestone quarries loaded boats and he was crushed between the two boats. The weather remained icy when on 4 January 1841 William Barnacle was killed when he fell from his boat, the *Crown Prince*, in Lock 7 of Hatton flight. Another child died at Hatton flight when the boat bashed hard into a lock and the toddler fell against the coal stove. Horrendously burnt, the lad's parents were both working the boat and didn't realise that the accident had happened until they reached the top of the flight, which took three hours.

One common crime is conspicuous by its absence; that of cruelty to horses. Wagoners and carriers were frequently arraigned for abusing their horses and, once the tramway opened, horses were often run down by the wagons behind them. There is not one instance of a boat horse being ill-treated.

Overall it seems remarkable that so few boatmen were killed considering the huge volume of traffic that the Stratford Canal carried during its first fifty years. The records of the coroner are very thorough, encompassing any death other than that of natural causes. It is a horrific catalogue of little understood illnesses whose results are described as 'Visitation of God', and shows only a gradual evolution towards our modern, more scientific, ways of thought. These records, and those of the various magistrates, provide an excellent insight into the early world of our canal system and its place in the wider social order.

CHAPTER 18

Odd Ends

The body was then gibbeted by the road as a stark and stern warning.

The history of Stratford-upon-Avon and South Warwickshire is crammed full of all sorts of odd little snippets about dark deeds; and, to be honest it, is pretty depressing going through this seemingly endless catalogue of violence and discord. Every now and then there are lighter moments though.

Oddly enough, you don't have to break up your marriage with a shotgun or hatchet. Back in the nineteenth century there was another option; you could always sell your wife. In a small town like Southam it not only sorted out the marital differences but created a whole day's entertainment too.

Indeed in 1806 it created a complete riot. Richard Cleaver, a penniless agricultural labourer was completely fed up with his wife Mary. If he had been a Lord or Viscount he could have divorced her by getting an Act of Parliament, but that really wasn't an option for Richard. It seems that Mary had been getting far too friendly with another labourer by the name of George Whitehead and so Richard decided to do things the old fashioned way.

On Saturday, when the market was in full swing, he tied a halter round her waist and dragged her into the market place and started the auction. Mayhem ensued as all the respectable gentry found their stalls crowded out of business, the road blocked by the milling crowd of labourers, and the pubs doing magnificent trade. For half an hour Richard 'did commit violent and enormous outrages' exhibiting his wife in a most unbecoming manner and eventually delivering her to George Whitehead. Alas the records of the day failed to say how much George paid for her, the usual price was a shilling. It may have been somewhat demeaning for poor old Mary, but it has to be better than being murdered.

William Palmer of Snitterfield was not so generous when he decided to sort out his marriage. The records for 1800 are very sparse, but the sorry tale was recorded in Thomas Hill's diary in between a detailed record of the weather. November was unbelievably wet. The river rose until it was half way up Bridge Street, both ends of Clopton Bridge were under water and the bodies of sheep and pigs were washed past the Church in ever increasing numbers. As the waters subsided on the 17th it wasn't just the bloated carcases of livestock that were revealed. At Grange Mill the body of a woman was found lodged in the flotsam. This was no accident; her throat had been cut.

The next day an inquest was opened and the body was identified as that of Mrs Palmer from the village of Snitterfield. The inquest decided that she had almost certainly been killed by her husband; but he was nowhere to be found. No doubt Palmer hoped that dumping the body in the swollen river would dispose of his wife quite thoroughly. When it was discovered he made a run for it.

Cranhill was the place where Palmer's body was gibbeted. The site was chosen because it was close to the scene of the murder and where it would be a very visible deterrent to anyone else contemplating murdering his wife. The author

Palmer got as far as Kings Norton before he was caught. He was brought back to Stratford in chains and then sent to Warwick gaol on 20 November. The local investigation took a while, but revealed this was no sudden outburst but a carefully planned murder in which both Palmer's sister and mother were involved. They were arrested on the 30th and joined William in the gaol. William's mother was released, but in the Lent Assizes both Palmer and his sister were found guilty of murder.

Wednesday 1 April 1801 saw them face the executioner. They were both hung at Warwick. William Palmer's body was cut down after an hour and carted to Cranhill Leas, close to where the crime was committed. The body was then gibbeted by the road as a stark and stern warning. Palmer's sister's body was given to the local doctor, Mr Gamble. He had a property near the Warwick Road and Thomas Hill called by to watch him dissect her body in the interests of science.

The Civil War

The Civil War altered Stratford forever. Whether the stories of the war are foul or suspicious enough for this book, or even criminal, I'll leave to the reader to decide. The driving force of the change to the town was not so much the battles and armies that surrounded the district but some of the characters involved. In a world turned upside down characters that should have stayed at the bottom of the pile floated to the top. Using the Royalist cause as a licence for banditry Colonel Wagstaffe blew the heart out of the town, whilst on the other hand, a Worcestershire farmer discovered Stratford was the ideal place for his visions of a modern utopia and launched not just the town, but the entire nation onto the path of modern industrial society; and he came to a premature and violent end too.

Andrew Yarranton was a dynamic character and thoroughly outspoken in his views. It was a combination that led him to a sticky end. He was born in 1616 to a farming family at Astley, Worcestershire. The family were devout Presbyterians, a significant factor in his political and industrial opinions. On 23 March 1642 Prince Rupert's army marched through Astley, forcibly seizing not only corn, but also impressing any able bodied men they could find. They didn't find many since Yarranton and many others had fled into the depths of Shrawley Wood. The increasingly anti royalist farmers of Worcestershire had enough, declaring '…we have been exposed by the outrages and violence of the soldiers threatening to fire our houses, to ravish our wives and daughters, and menacing our persons, we are now forced to associate ourselves in a mutual league for each others defence'. One thousand irate farmers voted Andrew Yarranton as their

Andrew Yarranton had grandiose plans to make Stratford the country's first industrial town. Here at Bridgefoot he wanted to build a vast complex of linen weaving sheds and looms powered by the river. Shakespeare Birthplace Trust Record Office

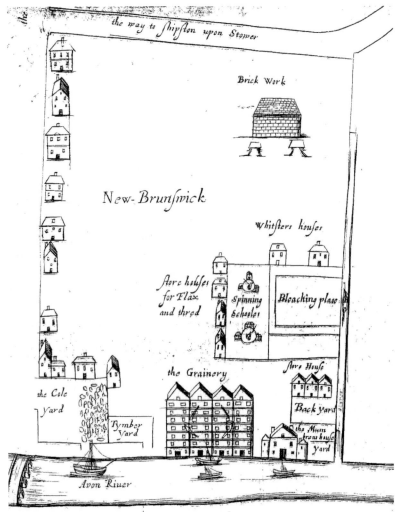

Captain. The local militia soon foiled a plot by the Royalists to seize a number of strategic manors, and once Cromwell's army arrived, they so harassed the Royalists that they were routed at the Battle of Worcester. Yarranton was awarded £500 by Parliament. Retiring from his unexpected military career, he used the windfall to start his own iron works at Astley.

The venture was an immediate success. Although the Civil War had seen the destruction of many bridges, towns such as Stratford, Pershore and Evesham were making strenuous efforts to reopen them. With the furnaces open in 1652, Andrew Yarranton started yet another venture in 1654, a linen manufactory. Apart from the simple profit motive, his staunch Presbyterian values always encouraged him to look for ways to enable other people, the poor in particular, to better their own lot in life by giving them the opportunity to work.

Charles II regained the throne and people who thrived during the inter-regnum were viewed with deep suspicion. Yarranton, notoriously hostile to the Royalist cause, was an immediate suspect. On 13 November 1660 he was arrested for treason and imprisoned at Worcester. His imprisonment ended amid a riot. 'The town was in an uproar and people crowded before the chamber to know what the matter was. I then told them how I and others were wrongfully imprisoned.' He had smashed open the windows of his cell to gain their attention. Shortly afterwards he was released and no more was said about the trumped up treason charges.

In Yarranton's view war had produced nothing but further suffering and increased trade was the only solution. He was not in the least frightened of speaking his mind on the subject, and found himself in brawls as a result. Where ever he went he saw the dilapidated state of English commerce and industry and how simple it would be to improve matters with a few harbours and manufactories. Yarranton realised that something had to be done on a national scale. He began work on his solution to the problems besetting the country.

England's Improvement by Sea and Land was published in 1677. It was a synthesis of all his experiences. A large section is dedicated to his proposals for linking the Upper Avon to the Thames via a canal and the river Cherwell, for the construction of granaries and improvements to England's seaports, particularly London. He proposed a Land Registry and a Central Bank of England. He went on to design a system for the manufacture of linen, using water powered looms and concentrating all the manufacture processes onto a single site. He was inventing the factory system in all but name. The first volume of *England's Improvement* is the route plan for the growth of England into a modern nation. He believed that Stratford would be at the very heart of this new industrial age.

Andrew Yarranton's visionary career came to an abrupt end in London in 1684. Once again he got into an argument, probably over religion, and resorted to using his fists. This time he was outnumbered and beaten thoroughly; he was

At Milcote Yarranton planned a series of granaries that would help eliminate the regular famines that killed thousands of poor peasants. His untimely murder ended all these schemes. Shakespeare Birthplace Trust Records Office

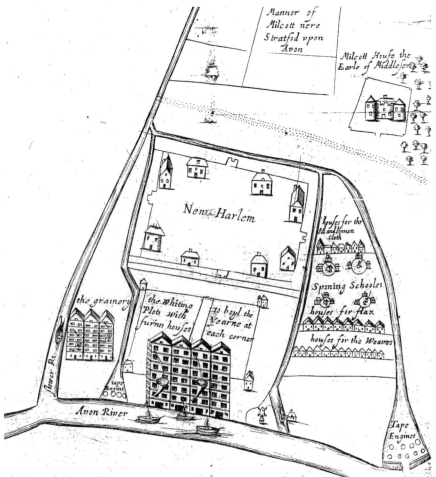

tipped into a water butt and apparently held down until he drowned. His turbulent life reflected the anarchic times of England's Civil War and the Restoration, but his ideas sowed the seeds of the Industrial Revolution.

If Andrew Yarranton represented the positive outcome of the Civil War in Stratford, Colonel Joseph Wagstaffe showed everyone just how two-faced and rapacious the alternative was. Wagstaffe was born in Harbury, the other side of Leamington, in 1611. By the outbreak of the Civil War in 1642 he was serving in the Irish Regiment in France with the rank of Major. He was recalled to England and promoted to Lieutenant Colonel on 6 July with instructions to raise an army for the suppression of the Irish. Quite what the Irishmen of his previous regiment thought of this is unrecorded. The Irish adventure never took place as the King effectively declared war on Parliament that September. Joseph Wagstaffe was placed in charge of two regiments of Parliamentary troops; it was a mistake. The Puritan troops were nothing if not God-fearing, righteous men and did not view the womanising drunken antics of their Lieutenant Colonel with approval. Wagstaffe was in it for the booty, the booze and the birds; they were there to fight for Parliament and a new Godly society. Within a few months they had managed to leave him on a battlefield to be captured by the Royalists. If they hadn't been so saintly he would probably have been shot in the back.

Wagstaffe didn't stay a prisoner for long; his natural tendencies towards drunken debauchery endeared him to the Royalists, and they promptly gave him a troop of 200 Cavalry and sent him off to create mayhem. This unruly mob occupied Stratford in January 1643. The Parliamentary forces of Lord Brooke at Warwick got wind of this and started to march towards the town. For a while it looked as though the town would be the scene of the battle. Luckily Stratford is impossible to defend. It has never had walls and is situated in a valley, completely vulnerable to cannon fire. Wagstaffe realised his cavalry horses would get trapped in the streets and moved his little army out towards the Welcombe Hills to spy out the advancing forces. The very heavy rain had made the ground soft and both sides found the going hard. Lord Brooke spotted Wagstaffe's horses and a preliminary skirmish proved nothing except the ground was too wet to gallop on. Rather than engage in pitched battle, Lord Brooke used a barrage of cannon fire against Wagstaffe as soon as he was in range. The effect was instant and dramatic. 'From the reer division we let flie a drake, which ran through the midst of them', wrote one witness; 'and forced them to wheele off towards the town and we hasted after them as fast as our carriages and the plowd lands so well softened with the raine would permit us.'

Most of Wagstaffe's horses not only retreated to the town, but kept on riding. Wagstaffe himself went into hiding to see what more mischief he could make. It wasn't long before he spotted the perfect opportunity. Lord Brooke was confident that Stratford was now secure and arranged a council of war in the Town Hall. In those days it was open on the ground floor, where there was an ammunition store and upstairs was the room in which the leading Parliamentary generals were to meet. Wagstaffe devised an astonishingly audacious plan. He crept unseen into the Town Hall, laid a trail of gunpowder into the barrels and set a timed match to detonate all the explosives once all the generals were gathered upstairs.

It very nearly worked. Brooke and the other generals were walking down the High Street towards the Hall when it exploded. Wagstaffe had timed the fuse a fraction too early. The Town Hall was completely demolished, one man was killed outright and four others so seriously burnt that they very nearly died. Wagstaffe fled from the town never to return. He had been within an inch of destroying the entire Parliamentary Army High Command and altering the entire course of the English Civil War.

The Civil War was a dreadful period in English history, but throughout the centuries the people of South Warwickshire have endeavoured to make their lives just as difficult. It is hard to know quite when to bring this book to an end, there are so many instances of sheer malice if not actual murder. One of the most hideous assaults to my mind was that of John Handcock on his wife Mary in 1837. This odious apology for a man had been in trouble with magistrates several times for threatening to shove Mary into the river. On 4 August he went into a chemist in Stratford and purchased an ounce of Oil of Vitriol, a ferociously powerful acid. He hid this at his home in Alveston until one in the morning on the 7th. Then, whilst Mary was peacefully asleep, he poured the acid onto her crotch. The acid burnt through her shift, her petticoat and inflicted the most horrific injuries. She awoke in agony. John Handcock refused to call a doctor and hid the bottle in the privy. Mary's screams were loud enough to rouse the entire village and medical help did eventually arrive, but not soon enough to prevent her being permanently scarred. John Handcock was found guilty and sentenced to two years' hard labour. He was yet another loathsome creature to enter the annals of Stratford's criminal history.

Appendix and Sources

Confession of Patrick Welch 2nd March 1796

The voluntary confession of Patrick Welch taken 2nd March 1796 in front of Marmaduke Matthews, Clerk of one of his magesty's justices of the peace in and for the said county this 2nd March 1796.

Who confesses that he was on guard last Christmas and had order from the Captain (Sherlock) to go patrolling at 9 o'clock and again at 12 o'clock, went at 9 and patrolled the streets and went into every public house to see that the men were in their quarters, at half past 9 returned to the guard house, went afterwards about 10 o'clock to his own quarters & called for a pot of beer but was refused by the landlady who told him it was too late, went from there to the Shakespeare where he found James Fitzgerald and Francis Quin & Thomas Cain, asked for a pot of beer but Quin said he should not have it, asked Quin if he was landlord of the house, he got in a passion left Quin's company and went down into the kitchen and got a pot of beer there in company with Fitzgerald and Hugh Kelley. From there went to the Malt Shovel where found plates and dishes lying broke on the floor, asked the landlady how they became broke who replied it was some of the soldiers and townsfolk who took her husband to prison, he bid the landlady not to be afraid as they would not hurt her husband and that she would have her husband back again in the morning, that if he did not affront any of them they would not do him any harm. He then asked her if she would trust him with a pot of beer till morning, but she refused saying she would not, she said she would.

Deponent further says

A common girl in the house called Miss Kitty which Kelley took into the yard went into a small house in the yard, he followed Kelley into the yard, called at the door of the house and asked Kelley to let him in, said he would in a few minutes, and then heard a noise in the street, went out where he saw James Kelley running after a man and woman with a drawn sword in his

*hand, he cried Come back, don't strike the woman, and followed
James Kelley as fast as he could till the man, woman and James
Kelley turned into a garden, that he lost sight of them and did not
know where they went. He met Irwin, asked him if he saw James
Kelley and the man and woman and told him that Kelley had a
broad sword drawn in his hand. Immediately heard the woman
shouting murder, when Irwin and he went in to see what was the
matter, found James Kelley striking the man with his sword. He
asked Kelley if he meant to take the mans life, went to Kelley and
pushed him away, brought him away about a yard and a half,
James Kelley slipt away from him and swore the man would do
better with another blow, then returned to the man and gave him
another blow on the head, he & Irwin took James Kelley to his
quarters* [White Lion] *where they left him.*

* the mark of Patrick Welch

Samuel Irwin's confession, 2nd March 1796 before Marmaduke Matthews

Who confesses that he was in his quarters at the White Lion at
Stratford upon Avon upon Christmas evening last when the
corporal [Ridley] went around the patrol and called him out
and desired him and Wm Howard to go with him into the
street and to go round with him to see the men's quarters,
telling them that Anderson had been knocked down and beat.
That Deponent and Howard accordingly went with the
corporal to the Malt Shovel where they found the landlord of
the house and took him into custody under a suspicion that he
was the person who had knocked down and beat Anderson.
That they took him to the guard house at the White Lion. That
the corporal went immediately and made his report to the
Captain [Redwood]. That while the Corporal Ridley was gone
to the Captain with his report, this deponent went from the
guard house into the street [leaving the landlord of the *Malt
Shovel* in the guard house]. That on his way towards the Malt
Shovel he met with Patrick Welch [one of his comrades] who
asked this deponent 'if he had seen James Kelly run after a
man and woman with a naked sword?' Deponent answered
him 'He did not'. Immediately after they heard a noise and ꝉ'

voice of a woman crying out Murder upon which this deponent and Welch immediately ran towards the place where the noise and cry came from – upon their coming near the place this deponent and Welch saw James Kelley beating a man with his naked sword as the man was lying on the ground. That Welch immediately ran up towards them and said to Kelley 'Damn your soul, do you mean to kill the man?' and laid hold of him. That Welch endeavoured to take him away and this deponent assisted him in so doing, that they brought him a small distance, not more than a few yards from the man but that he gave a sudden jerk and got away, having leaped from the hands of Welch when he gave himself a turn round and said "Damn me but he will do the better with another blow" and then turned back to the man who was still lying on the ground in the garden and struck him violently on the head with his drawn sword, that this deponent & Welch came up to him again and laid hold of Kelly and dragged him away to the guard house where they left him, Deponent went into his quarters leaving Welch at the guard house.

* The mark of Samuel Irwin

Sources

(1) Newspapers

Stratford upon Avon Herald & South Warwickshire Advertiser, 1860+
Warwickshire Advertiser, 1802+

(2) Books

Stratford upon Avon, Portrait of a Town, Nicholas Fog, Phillimore & Co Ltd, 1986
History of an English Borough, Stratford upon Avon 1196-1996, Edited by Robert Bearman, Sutton Publishing, 1997
The Borough Town of Stratford upon Avon, Levi Fox, MA, FSA, OBE, Corporation of Stratford, 1953
Archaeology and Development in Stratford upon Avon, T R Slater & C Wilson, University of Birmingham, 1977

Index